Some Thoughts Concerning Education.

John Locke

1914

This book has been published by:

Contact: sales@nuvisionpublications.com
URL: http://www.nuvisionpublications.com

Publishing Date: 2007

ISBN# 1-59547-834-5

Please see our website for several books created for
education, research and entertainment.

Specializing in rare, out-of-print books still in demand.

Contents

Introductory Note

JOHN LOCKE was born near Bristol, England, on August 29, 1632; and was educated at Westminster School, where Dryden was his contemporary, and at Christ Church, Oxford. Of the discipline then in vogue in either institution, the future educational theorist had no high opinion, as may be gathered from allusions in the present treatise; yet, after taking his master's degree in 1658, he became tutor of his college, and lecturer in Greek and rhetoric. After a visit to the Continent in 1665, as secretary to an embassy, he returned to Oxford and took up the study of medicine. He became attached, as friend and physician, to Lord Ashley, afterward the first Earl of Shaftesbury; and while this nobleman was Lord Chancellor, Locke held the office of Secretary of Presentations.

Shaftesbury went out of office in 1673, and two years later Locke went to France in search of health, supporting himself by acting as tutor to the son of Sir John Banks, and as physician to the wife of the English Ambassador at Paris. In 1679, Shaftesbury, being again in power, recalled Locke to England. He reluctantly obeyed, and remained in attendance on his patron, assisting him in political matters and superintending the education of his grandson, the future author of "Characteristics," till Shaftesbury's political fortunes finally collapsed, and both men took refuge in Holland.

Locke's first two years in Holland were spent in traveling and in intercourse with scholars; but in 1685 the Dutch Government was asked to deliver him up to the English as a traitor, and he was forced to go into hiding till a pardon was granted by James II in 1686, though there is no evidence of his having been guilty of any crime beyond his friendship with Shaftesbury.

It was not till now, at the age of fifty-four, that Locke began to publish the results of a lifetime of study and thought. An epitome of his great "Essay Concerning Human Understanding" was printed in his friend Le Clerc's "Bibliothèque Universelle," and the work was finally published in full in 1690. It was from Holland also that he wrote, as advice to a friend on the bringing up of his son, those letters which were later printed as "Thoughts Concerning Education."

During his exile Locke had come into friendly relations with his future sovereigns, William and Mary; and when the Revolution was accomplished he came back to England with the Princess in 1689. He was offered the Ambassadorship to Prussia, but declined on account of his weak health and because he thought he was not valiant enough in strong drink to be Ambassador at the court of the Elector of Brandenburg; so he stayed at home and published his "Essay."

The remainder of his life was spent chiefly at the home of his friends, the Cudworths and Mashams, at Oates in Essex. He held the office of Commissioner of Appeals, and was for some years a member of the Council of Trade and Plantations, a position which led to his occupying himself with problems of economics. At Oates he had the opportunity of putting his educational theories into practise in the training of the grandson of his host, and the results confirmed his belief in his methods. He died at Oates, October 27, 1704.

It has been noted that while at school and at the university Locke disapproved the educational methods employed; and this independence of judgment marked him through life. In medicine he denounced the scholasticism which still survived and which in various branches of learning had already been attacked by Bacon and Hobbes; and he advocated the experimental methods adopted by his friend Sydenham, the great physician of the day. In educational theory and method he held advanced opinions, insisting especially on the importance of guarding the formation of habits, and on training in wisdom and virtue rather than on information as the main object of education. Many of his ideas are still among the objects aimed at, rather than achieved, by educational reformers. It will be observed from the following "Thoughts" that they bear the mark of their original purpose, the individual education of a gentleman's son, not the formation of a school system.

But it is as a philosopher that Locke's fame is greatest. He was the ancestor of the English empirical school, and he exercised a profound influence on philosophic thought throughout Europe. Almost all the main lines of the intellectual activity of the eighteenth century in England lead back to Locke, and the skepticism of Hume is the logical development of the principles laid down in the "Essay Concerning Human Understanding."

Dedication

TO EDWARD CLARKE, of Chipley, Esq.

SIR:THESE *thoughts concerning education,* which now come abroad into the world, do of right belong to you, being written several years since for your sake, and are no other than what you have already by you in my letters. I have so little vary'd any thing, but only the order of what was sent you at different times, and on several occasions, that the reader will easily find, in the familiarity and fashion of the stile, that they were rather the private conversation of two friends, than a discourse design'd for publick view.

The importunity of friends is the common apology for publications men are afraid to own themselves forward to. But you know I can truly say, that if some, who having heard of these papers of mine, had not press'd to see them, and afterwards to have them printed, they had lain dormant still in that privacy they were design'd for. But those, whose judgment I defer much to, telling me, that they were persuaded, that this rough draught of mine might be of some use, if made more publick, touch'd upon what will always be very prevalent with me: for I think it every man's indispensable duty, to do all the service he can to his country; and I see not what difference he puts between himself and his cattle, who lives without that thought. This subject is of so great concernment, and a right way of education is of so general advantage, that did I find my abilities answer my wishes, I should not have needed exhortations or importunities from others. However, the meanness of these papers, and my just distrust of them, shall not keep me, by the shame of doing so little, from contributing my mite, when there is no more requir'd of me than my throwing it into the publick receptacle. And if there be any more of their size and notions, who lik'd them so well, that they thought them worth printing, I may flatter myself they will not be lost labour to every body.

I myself have been consulted of late by so many, who profess themselves at a loss how to breed their children, and the early corruption of youth is now become so general a complaint, that he cannot be thought wholly impertinent, who brings the consideration of this matter on the stage, and offers something, if it be but to excite others, or afford matter of correction: for errors in education should be less indulg'd than any. These, like faults in the first concoction, that are never mended in the second or third, carry their afterwards incorrigible taint with them thro' all the parts and stations of life.

I am so far from being conceited of any thing I have here offer'd, that I should not be sorry, even for your sake, if some one abler and fitter for such a task would in a just treatise of education, suited to our *English* gentry, rectify the mistakes I have made in this; it being much more desirable to me, that young gentlemen should be put into (that which every one ought to be solicitous about) the best way of being form'd and instructed, than that my opinion should be receiv'd concerning it. You will, however, in the mean time bear me witness, that the method here propos'd has had no ordinary effects upon a gentleman's son it was not design'd for. I will not say the good temper of the child did not very much contribute to it; but this I think you and the parents are satisfy'd of, that a contrary usage, according to the ordinary disciplining of children, would not have mended that temper, nor have brought him to be in love with his book, to take a pleasure in learning, and to desire, as he does, to be taught more than those about him think fit always to teach him.

But my business is not to recommend this treatise to you, whose opinion of it I know already; nor it to the world, either by your opinion or patronage. The well educating of their children is so much the duty and concern of parents, and the welfare and prosperity of the nation so much depends on it, that I would have every one lay it seriously to heart; and after having well examin'd and distinguish'd what fancy, custom, or reason advises in the case, set his helping hand to promote every where that way of training up youth, with regard to their several conditions, which is the easiest, shortest, and likeliest to produce virtuous, useful, and able men in their distinct callings; tho' that most to be taken care of is the gentleman's calling. For if those of that rank are by their education once set right, they will quickly bring all the rest into order.

I know not whether I have done more than shewn my good wishes towards it in this short discourse; such as it is, the world now has it, and if there be any thing in it worth their acceptance, they owe their thanks to you for it. My affection to you gave the first rise to it, and I am pleas'd, that I can leave to posterity this mark of the friendship that has been between us. For I know no greater pleasure in this life, nor a better remembrance to be left behind one, than a long continued friendship with an honest, useful, and worthy man, and lover of his country. I am, Sir, Your most humble and most faithful servant,

JOHN LOCKE.
March 7, 1692.
[i.e. 169 2/3].

Sections 1–10

1. A Sound mind in a sound body, is a short, but full description of a happy state in this world. He that has these two, has little more to wish for; and he that wants either of them, will be but little the better for any thing else. Men's happiness or misery is most part of their own making. He, whose mind directs not wisely, will never take the right way; and he, whose body is crazy and feeble, will never be able to advance in it. I confess, there are some men's constitutions of body and mind so vigorous, and well fram'd by nature, that they need not much assistance from others; but by the strength of their natural genius, they are from their cradles carried towards what is excellent; and by the privilege of their happy constitutions, are able to do wonders. But examples of this kind are but few; and I think I may say, that of all the men we meet with, nine parts of ten are what they are, good or evil, useful or not, by their education. 'Tis that which makes the great difference in mankind. The little, or almost insensible impressions on our tender infancies, have very important and lasting consequences: and there 'tis, as in the fountains of some rivers, where a gentle application of the hand turns the flexible waters in channels, that make them take quite contrary courses; and by this direction given them at first in the source, they receive different tendencies, and arrive at last at very remote and distant places.

2. I imagine the minds of children as easily turn'd this or that way, as water it self: and though this be the principal part, and our main care should be about the inside, yet the clay-cottage is not to be neglected. I shall therefore begin with the case, and consider first the *health* of the body, as that which perhaps you may rather expect from that study I have been thought more peculiarly to have apply'd my self to; and that also which will be soonest dispatch'd, as lying, if I guess not amiss, in a very little compass.

3. How necessary *health* is to our business and happiness; and how requisite a strong constitution, able to endure hardships and fatigue, is to one that will make any figure in the world, is too obvious to need any proof.

4. The consideration I shall here have of *health,* shall be, not what a physician ought to do with a sick and crazy child; but what the parents, without the help of physick, should do for the *preservation and improvement of an healthy,* or at least *not sickly constitution* in their children. And this perhaps might be all dispatch'd in this one short rule, *viz.* That gentlemen should use their children, as the honest farmers and substantial yeomen do theirs. But because the mothers possibly may think this a little too hard, and the fathers too short, I shall explain my self more particularly; only laying down this as a general and certain observation for the women to consider, *viz.* That most children's constitutions are either spoil'd, or at least harm'd, by cockering and tenderness.

5. The first thing to be taken care of, is, that children be not too *warmly clad or cover'd,* winter or summer. The face when we are born, is no less tender than any other part of the body. 'Tis use alone hardens it, and makes it more able to endure the cold. And therefore the *Scythian* philosopher gave a very significant answer to the *Athenian,* who wonder'd how he could go naked in frost and snow. *How,* said the *Scythian, can you endure your face expos'd to the sharp winter air? My face is us'd to it,* said the *Athenian. Think me all face,* reply'd the *Scythian.* Our bodies will endure any thing, that from the beginning they are accustom'd to.

An eminent instance of this, though in the contrary excess of heat, being to our present purpose, to shew what use can do, I shall set down in the author's words, as I meet with it in a late ingenious voyage.

"The heats, says he, are more violent in Malta, than in any part of Europe: they exceed those of Rome itself, and are perfectly stifling; and so much the more, because there are seldom any cooling breezes here. This makes the common people as black as gypsies: but yet the peasants defy the sun; they work on in the hottest part of the day, without intermission, or sheltering themselves from his scorching rays. This has convinc'd me, that nature can bring itself to many things, which seem impossible, provided we accustom ourselves from our infancy. The Malteses do so, who harden the bodies of their children, and reconcile them to the heat, by making them go stark naked, without shirt, drawers, or any thing on their heads, from their cradles till they are ten years old."

Give me leave therefore to advise you not to fence too carefully against the cold of this our climate. There are those in *England,* who wear the same clothes winter and summer, and that without any inconvenience, or more sense of cold than others find. But if the mother will needs have an allowance for frost and snow, for fear of harm, and the father, for fear of censure, be sure let not his winter clothing be too warm: And amongst other things, remember, that when nature has so well covered his head with hair, and strengthen'd it with a year or two's age, that he can run about by day without a cap, it is best that by night

12

a child should also lie without one; there being nothing that more exposes to headaches, colds, catarrhs, coughs, and several other diseases, than keeping the *head warm.*

6. I have said *he* here, because the principal aim of my discourse is, how a young gentleman should be brought up from his infancy, which in all things will not so perfectly suit the education of *daughters;* though where the difference of sex requires different treatment, 'twill be no hard matter to distinguish.

7. I will also advise his *feet to be wash'd* every day in cold water, and to have his *shoes* so thin, that they might leak and *let in water,* whenever he comes near it. Here, I fear I shall have the mistress and maids too against me. One will think it too filthy, and the other perhaps too much pains, to make clean his stockings. But yet truth will have it, that his health is much more worth than all such considerations, and ten times as much more. And he that considers how mischievous and mortal a thing taking *wet in the feet* is, to those who have been bred nicely, will wish he had, with the poor people's children, gone *bare-foot,* who, by that means, come to be so reconcil'd by custom to wet in their feet, that they take no more cold or harm by it, than if they were wet in their hands. And what is it, I pray, that makes this great difference between the hands and the feet in others, but only custom? I doubt not, but if a man from his cradle had been always us'd to go bare-foot, whilst his hands were constantly wrapt up in warm mittins, and cover'd with *hand-shoes,* as the *Dutch* call *gloves;* I doubt not, I say, but such a custom would make taking wet in his hands as dangerous to him, as now taking wet in their feet is to great many others. The way to prevent this, is, to have his shoes made so as to leak water, and his feet wash'd constantly every day in cold water. It is recommendable for its cleanliness; but that which I aim at in it, is health; and therefore I limit it not precisely to any time of the day. I have known it us'd every night with very good success, and that all the winter, without the omitting it so much as one night in extreme cold weather; when thick ice cover'd the water, the child bathed his legs and feet in it, though he was of an age not big enough to rub and wipe them himself, and when he began this custom was puling and very tender. But the great end being to harden those parts by a frequent and familiar use of cold water, and thereby to prevent the mischiefs that usually attend accidental taking wet in the feet in those who are bred otherwise, I think it may be left to the prudence and convenience of the parents, to chuse either night or morning. The time I deem indifferent, so the thing be effectually done. The health and hardiness procured by it, would be a good purchase at a much dearer rate. To which if I add the preventing of corns, that to some men would be a very valuable consideration. But begin first in the spring with luke-warm, and so colder and colder every time, till in a few days you come to perfectly cold water, and then continue it so winter and summer. For it is to be observed in this, as in all other *alterations* from our ordinary way of living, the changes must be made by gentle

and insensible degrees; and so we may bring our bodies to any thing, without pain, and without danger.

How fond mothers are like to receive this doctrine, is not hard to foresee. What can it be less, than to murder their tender babes, to use them thus? What! put their feet in cold water in frost and snow, when all one can do is little enough to keep them warm? A little to remove their fears by examples, without which the plainest reason is seldom hearken'd to: *Seneca* tells us of himself, *Ep.* 53, and 83, that he used to bathe himself in cold spring-water in the midst of winter. This, if he had not thought it not only tolerable, but healthy too, he would scarce have done, in an exorbitant fortune, that could well have borne the expence of a warm bath, and in an age (for he was then old) that would have excused greater indulgence. If we think his stoical principles led him to this severity, let it be so, that this sect reconciled cold water to his sufferance. What made it agreeable to his health? For that was not impair'd by this hard usage. But what shall we say to *Horace,* who warm'd not himself with the reputation of any sect, and least of all affected stoical austerities? yet he assures us, he was wont in the winter season to bathe himself in cold water. But, perhaps, *Italy* will be thought much warmer than *England,* and the chillness of their waters not to come near ours in winter. If the rivers of *Italy* are warmer, those of *Germany* and *Poland* are much colder, than any in this our country, and yet in these, the *Jews,* both men and women, bathe all over, at all seasons of the year, without any prejudice to their health. And every one is not apt to believe it is miracle, or any peculiar virtue of St. *Winifred's* Well, that makes the cold waters of that famous spring do no harm to the tender bodies that bathe in it. Every one is now full of the miracles done by cold baths on decay'd and weak constitutions, for the recovery of health and strength; and therefore they cannot be impracticable or intolerable for the improving and hardening the bodies of those tho are in better circumstances.

If these examples of grown men be not thought yet to reach the case of children, but that they may be judg'd still to be too tender, and unable to bear such usage, let them examine what the *Germans* of old, and the Irish now, do to them, and they will find, that infants too, as tender as they are thought, may, without any danger, endure bathing, not only of their feet, but of their whole bodies, in cold water. And there are, at this day, ladies in the Highlands of *Scotland* who use this discipline to their children in the midst of winter, and find that cold water does them no harm, even when there is ice in it.

8. I shall not need here to mention *swimming,* when he is of an age able to learn, and has any one to teach him. 'Tis that saves many a man's life; and the *Romans* thought it so necessary, that they rank'd it with letters; and it was the common phrase to mark one ill-educated, and good for nothing, that he had neither learnt to read nor to swim: *Nec literas didicit nec natare.* But, besides the gaining a skill which may serve him at need, the advantages to health by often *bathing in cold*

water during the heat of summer, are so many, that I think nothing need be said to encourage it; provided this one caution be us'd, that he never go into the water when exercise has at all warm'd him, or left any emotion in his blood or pulse.

9. Another thing that is of great advantage to every one's health, but especially children's, is to be much in the *open air,* and as little as may be by the fire, even in winter. By this he will accustom himself also to heat and cold, shine and rain; all which if a man's body will not endure, it will serve him to very little purpose in this world; and when he is grown up, it is too late to begin to use him to it. It must be got early, and by degrees. Thus the body may be brought to bear almost any thing. If I should advise him to play in the *wind and sun without a hat,* I doubt whether it could be borne. There would a thousand objections be made against it, which at last would amount to no more, in truth, than being sun-burnt. And if my young master be to be kept always in the shade, and never expos'd to the sun and wind for fear of his complexion, it may be a good way to make him a *beau,* but not a man of business. And altho' greater regard be to be had to beauty in the daughters; yet I will take the liberty to say, that the more they are in the *air,* without prejudice to their faces, the stronger and healthier they will be; and the nearer they come to the hardships of their brothers in their education, the greater advantage will they receive from it all the remaining part of their lives.

10. Playing in the *open air* has but this one danger in it, that I know; and that is, that when he is hot with running up and down, he should sit or lie down on the cold or moist earth. This I grant; and drinking cold drink, when they are hot with labour or exercise, brings more people to the grave, or to the brink of it, by fevers, and other diseases, than anything I know. These mischiefs are easily enough prevented whilst he is little, being then seldom out of sight. And if, during his childhood, he be constantly and rigorously kept form sitting on the ground, or drinking any cold liquor whilst he is hot, the custom of forbearing, grown into *habit,* will help much to preserve him, when he is no longer under his maid's or tutor's eye. This is all I think can be done in the case: for, as years increase, liberty must come with them; and in a great many things he must be trusted to his own conduct, since there cannot always be a guard upon him, except what you have put into his own mind by good principles, and establish'd habits, which is the best and surest, and therefore most to be taken care of. For, from repeated cautions and rules, never so often inculcated, you are not to expect any thing either in this, or any other case, farther than practice has establish'd them into habits.

Sections 11–20

11. One thing the mention of the girls brings into my mind, which must not be forgot; and that is, that your son's *clothes* be *never* made *strait,* especially about the breast. Let nature have scope to fashion the body as she thinks best. She works of herself a great deal better and exacter than we can direct her. And if women were themselves to frame the bodies of their children in their wombs, as they often endeavour to mend their shapes when they are out, we should as certainly have no perfect children born, as we have few well-shap'd that are *strait-lac'd,* or much tamper'd with. This consideration should, methinks, keep busy people (I will not say ignorant nurses and bodice-makers) from meddling in a matter they understand not; and they should be afraid to put nature out of her way in fashioning the parts, when they know not how the least and meanest is made. And yet I have seen so many instances of children receiving great harm from *strait-lacing,* that I cannot but conclude there are other creatures as well as monkeys, who, little wiser than they, destroy their young ones by senseless fondness, and too much embracing.

12. Narrow breasts, short and stinking breath, ill lungs, and crookedness, are natural and almost constant effects of *hard bodice,* and *clothes that pinch.* That way of making slender wastes, and fine shapes, serves but the more effectually to spoil them. Nor can there indeed but be disproportion in the parts, when the nourishment prepared in the several offices of the body cannot be distributed as nature designs. And therefore what wonder is it, if, it being laid where it can, on some part not so *braced,* it often makes a shoulder or hip higher or bigger than its just proportion? 'Tis generally known, that the women of *China,* (imagining I know not what kind of beauty in it) by bracing and binding them hard from their infancy, have very little feet. I saw lately a pair of *China* shoes, which I was told were for a grown woman: they were so exceedingly disproportion'd to the feet of one of the same age among us, that they would scarce have been big enough for one of our little girls. Besides this, 'tis observ'd, that their women are also very little, and short-liv'd; whereas the men are of the ordinary stature of other men, and live to a proportionable age. These defects in the female sex in that country, are by some imputed to the unreasonable binding of their feet, whereby the free circulation of the blood is hinder'd, and the growth and health of the whole body suffers. And how often do we see, that some small part of the foot being injur'd by a wrench or a blow, the whole leg or thigh thereby lose their strength and nourishment, and dwindle away? How much greater inconveniences may we expect, when

the *thorax,* wherein is placed the heart and seat of life, is unnaturally *compress'd,* and hinder'd from its due expansion?

13. As for his *diet,* it ought to be very plain and simple; and, if I might advise, flesh should be forborne as long as he is in coats, or at least till he is two or three years old. But whatever advantage this may be to his present and future health and strength, I fear it will hardly be consented to by parents, misled by the custom of eating too much flesh themselves, who will be apt to think their children, as they do themselves, in danger to be starv'd, if they have not flesh at least twice a-day. This I am sure, children would breed their teeth with much less danger, be freer from diseases whilst they were little, and lay the foundations of an healthy and strong constitution much surer, if they were not cramm'd so much as they are by fond mothers and foolish servants, and were kept wholly from flesh the first three or four years of their lives.

But if my young master must needs have flesh, let it be but once a day, and of one sort of a meal. Plain beef, mutton, veal, &c. without other sauce than hunger, is best; and great care should be used, that he eat *bread* plentifully, both alone and with every thing else; and whatever he eats that is solid, make him chew it well. We *English* are often negligent herein; from whence follow indigestion, and other great inconveniences.

14. For *breakfast* and *supper, milk, milk-pottage, water-gruel, flummery,* and twenty other things, that we are wont to make in *England,* are very fit for children; only, in all these, let care be taken that they be plain, and without much mixture, and very sparingly season'd with sugar, or rather none at all; especially *all spice,* and other things that may heat the blood, are carefully to be avoided. Be sparing also of *salt* in the seasoning of all his victuals, and use him not to high-season'd meats. Our palates grow into a relish and liking of the seasoning and cookery which by custom they are set to; and an over-much use of salt, besides that it occasions thirst, and over-much drinking, has other ill effects upon the body. I should think that a good piece of well-made and well-bak'd *brown bread,* sometimes with, and sometimes without *butter* or *cheese,* would be often the best breakfast for my young master. I am sure 'tis as wholesome, and will make him as strong a man as greater delicacies; and if he be used to it, it will be as pleasant to him. If he at any time calls for victuals between meals, use him to nothing but dry *bread.* If he be hungry more than wanton, *bread* alone will down; and if he be not hungry, 'tis not fit he should eat. By this you will obtain two good effects: 1. That by custom he will come to be in love with *bread;* for, as I said, our palates and stomachs too are pleased with the things we are used to. 2. Another good you will gain hereby is, that you will not teach him to eat more nor oftener than nature requires. I do not think that all people's appetites are alike; some have naturally stronger, and some weaker stomachs. But this I think, that many are made *gormands* and *gluttons* by custom, that were not

so by nature; and I see in some countries, men as lusty and strong, that eat but two meals a-day, as others that have set their stomachs by a constant usage, like larums, to call on them for four or five. The *Romans* usually fasted till supper, the only set meal even of those who eat more than once a-day; and those who us'd breakfast, as some did, at eight, some at ten, others at twelve of the clock, and some later, neither eat flesh, nor had any thing made ready for them. *Augustus,* when the greatest monarch on the earth, tells us, he took a bit of dry bread in his chariot. And *Seneca,* in his 83rd *Epistle,* giving an account how he managed himself, even when he was old, and his age permitted indulgence, says, that he used to eat a piece of dry bread for his dinner, without the formality of sitting to it, tho' his estate would as well have paid for a better meal (had health requir'd it) as any subject's in *England,* were it doubled. The masters of the world were bred up with this spare diet; and the young gentlemen of *Rome* felt no want of strength or spirit, because they eat but once a day. Or if it happen'd by chance, that any one could not fast so long as till supper, their only set meal, he took nothing but a bit of dry bread, or at most a few raisins, or some such slight thing with it, to stay his stomach. This part of temperance was found so necessary both for health and business, that the custom of only one meal a day held out against that prevailing luxury which their *Eastern* conquests and spoils had brought in amongst them; and those who had given up their old frugal eating, and made feasts, yet began them not till the evening. And more than one set meal a-day was thought so monstrous, that it was a reproach as low down as *Cæsar's* time, to make an entertainment, or sit down to a full table, till towards sun-set; and therefore, if it would not be thought too severe, I should judge it most convenient that my young master should have nothing but *bread* too for *breakfast.* You cannot imagine of what force custom is; and I impute a great part of our diseases in *England,* to our eating too much *flesh,* and too little *bread.*

15. As to his *meals,* I should think it best, that as much as it can be conveniently avoided, they should not be kept constantly to an hour: for when custom has fix'd his eating to certain stated periods, his stomach will expect victuals at the usual hour, and grow peevish if he passes it; either fretting itself into a troublesome excess, or flagging into a downright want of appetite. Therefore I would have no time kept constantly to for his breakfast, dinner and supper, but rather vary'd almost every day. And if betwixt these, which I call *meals,* he will eat, let him have, as often as he calls for it, good dry bread. If any one think this too hard and sparing a diet for a child, let them know, that a child will never starve nor dwindle for want of nourishment, who, besides flesh at dinner, and spoon-meat, or some such other thing, at supper, may have good bread and beer as often as he has a stomach. For thus, upon second thoughts, I should judge it best for children to be order'd. The morning is generally design'd for study, to which a full stomach is but an ill preparation. Dry bread, though the best nourishment, has the least temptation; and no body would have a child cramm'd at breakfast, who has any regard to his mind or body, and would not have him dull

and unhealthy. Nor let any one think this unsuitable to one of estate and condition. A gentleman in any age ought to be so bred, as to be fitted to bear arms, and be a soldier. But he that in this, breeds his son so, as if he design'd him to sleep over his life in the plenty and ease of a full fortune he intends to leave him, little considers the examples he has seen, or the age he lives in.

16. His *drink* should be only small beer; and that too he should never be suffer'd to have between meals, but after he had eat a piece of bread. The reasons why I say this are these.

17. I. More fevers and surfeits are got by people's drinking when they are hot, than by any one thing I know. Therefore, if by play he be hot and dry, bread will ill go down; and so if he cannot have *drink* but upon that condition, he will be forced to forbear; for, if he be very hot, he should by no means *drink*; at least a good piece of bread first to be eaten, will gain time to warm the beer *blood-hot,* which then he may drink safely. If he be very dry, it will go down so warm'd, and quench his thirst better; and if he will not drink it so warm'd, abstaining will not hurt him. Besides, this will teach him to forbear, which is an habit of greatest use for health of body and mind too.

18. 2. Not being permitted to *drink* without eating, will prevent the custom of having the cup often at his nose; a dangerous beginning, and preparation to *good-fellowship.* Men often bring habitual hunger and thirst on themselves by custom. And if you please to try, you may, though he be wean'd from it, bring him by use to such a necessity again of *drinking* in the night, that he will not be able to sleep without it. It being the lullaby used by nurses to still crying children, I believe mothers generally find some difficulty to wean their children from drinking in the night, when they first take them home. Believe it, custom prevails as much by day as by night; and you may, if you please, bring any one to be thirsty every hour.

I once liv'd in a house, where, to appease a forward child, they gave him *drink* as often as he cry'd; so that he was constantly bibbing. And tho' he could not speak, yet he drank more in twenty-four hours than I did. Try it when you please, you may with small, as well as with strong beer, drink your self into a drought. The great thing to be minded in education is, what *habits* you settle; and therefore in this, as all other things, do not begin to make any thing *customary,* the practice whereof you would not have continue and increase. It is convenient for health and sobriety, to *drink* no more than natural thirst requires; and he that eats not salt meats, nor drinks strong drink, will seldom thirst between meals, unless he has been accustom'd to such unseasonable *drinking.*

19. Above all, take great care that he seldom, if ever, taste any *wine* or *strong drink.* There is nothing so ordinarily given children in *England,* and nothing so destructive to them. They ought never to *drink* any *strong liquor* but when they need it as a cordial, and the doctor

20

prescribes it. And in this case it is, that servants are most narrowly to be watch'd and most severely to be reprehended when they transgress. Those mean sort of people, placing a great part of their happiness in *strong drink,* are always forward to make court to my young master by offering him that which they love best themselves: and finding themselves made merry by it, they foolishly think 'twill do the child no harm. This you are carefully to have your eye upon, and restrain with all the skill and industry you can, there being nothing that lays a surer foundation of mischief, both to body and mind than children's being us'd to *strong drink,* especially to drink in private *with the servants.*

20. *Fruit* makes one of the most difficult chapters in the government of health, especially that of children. Our first parents ventur'd *Paradise* for it; and 'tis no wonder our children cannot stand the temptation, tho' it cost them their health. The regulation of this cannot come under any one general rule; for I am by no means of their mind, who would keep children almost wholly from *fruit,* as a thing totally unwholesome for them; by which strict way, they make them but the more ravenous after it, and to eat good or bad, ripe or unripe, all that they can get, whenever they come at it. *Melons, peaches,* most sorts of *plums,* and all sorts of *grapes* in *England,* I think children should be *wholly kept from,* as having a very tempting taste, in a very unwholesome juice; so that if it were possible, they should never so much as see them, or know there were any such thing. But *strawberries, cherries, gooseberries,* or *currants,* when thorough ripe, I think may be very safely allow'd them, and that with a pretty liberal hand, if they be eaten with these cautions: 1. Not after meals, as we usually do, when the stomach is already full of other food: but I think they should be eaten rather before or between meals, and children should have them for their breakfast. 2. Bread eaten with them. 3. Perfectly ripe. If they are thus eaten, I imagine them rather conducing than hurtful to our health. *Summer-fruits,* being suited to the hot season of the year they come in, refresh our stomachs, languishing and fainting under it; and therefore I should not be altogether so strict in this point, as some are to their children; who being kept so very short, instead of a moderate quantity of well-chosen *fruit,* which being allow'd them would content them, whenever they can get loose, or bribe a servant to supply them, satisfy their longing with any trash they can get, and eat to a surfeit.

Apples and *pears* too, which are thorough ripe, and have been gather'd some time, I think may be safely eaten at any time, and in pretty large quantities, especially *apples;* which never did any body hurt, that I have heard, after *October.*

Fruits also dry'd without sugar, I think very wholesome. But *sweet-meats* of all kinds are to be avoided; which whether they do more harm to the maker or eater, is not easy to tell. This I am sure, it is one of the most inconvenient ways of expence that vanity hath yet found out; and so I leave them to the ladies.

Sections 21–30

21. Of all that looks soft and effeminate, nothing is more to be indulg'd children, than *sleep*. In this alone they are to be permitted to have their full satisfaction; nothing contributing more to the growth and health of children, than *sleep*. All that is to be regulated in it, is, in what part of the twenty-four hours they should take it; which will easily be resolved, by only saying that it is of great use to accustom 'em to rise early in the morning. It is best so to do, for health; and he that, from his childhood, has, by a settled custom, made *rising betimes* easy and familiar to him, will not, when he is a man, waste the best and most useful part of his life in drowsiness, and lying a-bed. If children therefore are to be call'd up early in the morning, it will follow of course, that they must go to bed betimes; whereby they will be accustom'd to avoid the unhealthy and unsafe hours of debauchery, which are those of the evenings; and they who keep good hours, seldom are guilty of any great disorders. I do not say this, as if your son, when grown up, should never be in company past eight, nor ever chat over a glass of wine 'till midnight. You are now, by the accustoming of his tender years, to indispose him to those inconveniences as much as you can; and it will be no small advantage, that contrary practice having made sitting up uneasy to him, it will make him often avoid, and very seldom propose midnight-revels. But if it should not reach so far, but fashion and company should prevail, and make him live as others do above twenty, 'tis worth the while to accustom him to *early rising* and early going to bed, between this and that, for the present improvement of his health and other advantages.

Though I have said, a large allowance of *sleep,* even as much as they will take, should be made to children when they are little; yet I do not mean, that it should always be continued to them in so large a proportion, and they suffer'd to indulge a drowsy laziness in their bed, as they grow up bigger. But whether they should begin to be restrained at seven or ten years old, or any other time, is impossible to be precisely determined. Their tempers, strength, and constitutions, must be consider'd. But some time between seven and fourteen, if they are too great lovers of their beds, I think it may be seasonable to begin to reduce them by degrees to about eight hours, which is generally rest enough for healthy grown people. If you have accustom'd him, as you should do, to rise constantly very early in the morning, this fault of being too long in bed will easily be reform'd, and most children will be forward enough to shorten that time themselves, by coveting to sit up with the company at night; tho' if they be not look'd after, they will be apt to take it out in the morning, which should by no means be permitted. They should constantly be call'd up and made to rise at their early hour; but great care should be taken in waking them, that it be not done hastily, nor with a loud or shrill voice, or any other sudden violent noise. This often affrights children, and does them great harm; and sound *sleep* thus broke off, with sudden alarms, is apt enough to discompose any one. When children are to be waken'd out of their *sleep,* be sure to begin with a low call, and some gentle motion, and so draw them out of it by degrees, and give them none but kind words and usage, 'till they are come perfectly to themselves, and being quite dress'd you are sure they are thoroughly awake. The being forc'd from their *sleep,* how gently so ever you do it, is pain enough to them; and care should be taken not to add any other uneasiness to it, especially such that may terrify them.

22. Let his *bed* be *hard,* and rather quilts than feathers. Hard lodging strengthens the parts; whereas being bury'd every night in feathers melts and dissolves the body, is often the cause of weakness, and forerunner of an early grave. And, besides the stone, which has often its rise from this warm wrapping of the reins, several other indispositions, and that which is the root of them all, a tender weakly constitution, is very much owing to *down-beds.* Besides, he that is used to hard lodging at home, will not miss his sleep (where he has most need of it) in his travels abroad, for want of his soft bed, and his pillows laid in order. And therefore, I think it would not be amiss, to *make his bed* after different fashions, sometimes lay his head higher, sometimes lower, that he may not feel every little change he must be sure to meet with, who is not design'd to lie always in my young master's bed at home, and to have his maid lay all things in print, and tuck him in warm. The great cordial of nature is *sleep.* He that misses that, will suffer by it; and he is very unfortunate, who can take his cordial only in his mother's fine gilt cup, and not in a wooden dish. He that can sleep soundly, takes the cordial; and it matters not whether it be on a soft *bed* or the hard boards. 'Tis *sleep* only that is the thing necessary.

23. One thing more there is, which has a great influence upon the health, and that is, *going to stool* regularly; people that are very *loose,* have seldom strong thoughts, or strong bodies. But the cure of this, both by diet and medicine, being much more easy than the contrary evil, there needs not much to be said about it; for if it come to threaten, either by its violence or duration, it will soon enough, and sometimes too soon, make a physician be sent for; and if it be moderate or short, it is commonly best to leave it to nature. On the other side, *costiveness* has too its ill effects, and is much harder to be dealt with by physick; purging medicines, which seem to give relief, rather increasing them than removing the evil.

24. It being an indisposition I had a particular reason to enquire into, and not finding the cure of it in books, I set my thoughts on work,

believing that greater changes than that might be made in our bodies, if we took the right course, and proceeded by rational steps.

1. Then I consider'd, that *going to stool,* was the effect of certain motions of the body; especially of the peristaltick motion of the guts.

2. I consider'd that several motions, that were not perfectly voluntary, might yet, by use and constant application, be brought to be habitual, if by an unintermitted custom they were at certain seasons endeavour'd to be constantly produced.

3. I had observ'd some men, who by taking after supper a pipe of tobacco, never fail'd of a *stool,* and began to doubt with myself, whether it were not more custom, than the tobacco, that gave them the benefit of nature; or at least, if the tobacco did it, it was rather by exciting a vigorous motion in the guts, than by any purging quality; for then it would have had other effects.

Having thus once got the opinion that it was possible to make it habitual, the next thing was to consider what way and means was the likeliest to obtain it.

4. Then I guess'd, that if a man, after his first eating in the morning, would presently solicit nature, and try whether he could strain himself so as to obtain a *stool,* he might in time, by constant application, bring it to be habitual.

25. The reasons that made me chuse this time, were,

1. Because the stomach being then empty, if it receiv'd any thing grateful to it (for I would never, but in case of necessity, have any one eat but what he likes, and when he has an appetite) it was apt to embrace it close by a strong constriction of its fibres; which constriction, I suppos'd, might probably be continu'd on in the guts, and so increase their peristaltick motion, as we see in the *Ileus,* that an inverted motion, being begun any where below, continues itself all the whole length, and makes even the stomach obey that irregular motion.

2. Because when men eat, they usually relax their thoughts, and the spirits then, free from other employments, are more vigorously distributed into the lower belly, which thereby contribute to the same effect.

3. Because, whenever men have leisure to eat, they have leisure enough also to make so much court to Madam *Cloacina,* as would be necessary to our present purpose; but else, in the variety of human affairs and accidents, it was impossible to affix it to any hour certain, whereby the custom would be interrupted. Whereas men in health seldom failing to eat once a day, tho' the hour chang'd, the custom might still be preserv'd.

26. Upon these grounds the experiment began to be try'd, and I have known none who have been steady in the prosecution of it, and taken care to go constantly to the necessary-house, after their first eating, whenever that happen'd, whether they found themselves call'd on or no, and there endeavoured to put nature upon her duty, but in a few months they obtain'd the desired success, and brought themselves to so regular an habit, that they seldom ever fail'd of a *stool* after their first eating, unless it were by their own neglect: for, whether they have any motion or no, if they go to the place, and do their part, they are sure to have nature very obedient.

27. I would therefore advise, that this course should be taken with a child every day presently after he has eaten his breakfast. Let him be set upon the stool, as if disburthening were as much in his power as filling his belly; and let not him or his maid know any thing to the contrary, but that it is so; and if he be forc'd to endeavour, by being hinder'd from his play or eating again 'till he has been effectually at *stool,* or at least done his utmost, I doubt not but in a little while it will become natural to him. For there is reason to suspect, that children being usually intent on their play, and very heedless of any thing else, often let pass those motions of nature, when she calls them but gently; and so they, neglecting the seasonable offers, do by degrees bring themselves into an habitual costiveness. That by this method costiveness may be prevented, I do more than guess; having known by the constant practice of it for some time, a child brought to have a *stool* regularly after his breakfast every morning.

28. How far any grown people will think fit to make trial of it, must be left to them; tho' I cannot but say, that considering the many evils that come from that defect, of a requisite easing of nature, I scarce know any thing more conducing to the preservation of health, than this is. Once in four and twenty hours, I think is enough; and no body, I guess, will think it too much. And by this means it is to be obtain'd without physick, which commonly proves very ineffectual in the cure of a settled and habitual costiveness.

29. This is all I have to trouble you with concerning his management in the ordinary course of his health. Perhaps it will be expected from me, that I should give some directions of *physick,* to prevent diseases; for which I have only this one, very sacredly to be observ'd, never to give children any *physick* for prevention. The observation of what I have already advis'd, will, I suppose, do that better than the ladies' diet-drinks or apothecaries' medicines. Have a great care of tampering that way, lest, instead of preventing, you draw on diseases. Nor even upon every little indisposition is *physick* to be given, or the physician to be call'd to children, especially if he be a busy man, that will presently fill their windows with gally-pots, and their stomachs with drugs. It is safer to leave them wholly to nature, than to put 'em into the hands of one forward to tamper, or that thinks children are to be cur'd, in ordinary

distempers, by any thing but diet, or by a method very little distant from it: it seeming suitable both to my reason and experience, that the tender constitutions of children should have as little done to them as is possible, and as the absolute necessity of the case requires. A little cold-still'd red *poppy-water*, which is the true surfeit-water with ease, and abstinence from flesh, often puts an end to several distempers in the beginning, which, by too forward applications, might have been made lusty diseases. When such a gentle treatment will not stop the growing mischief, nor hinder it from turning into a form'd disease, it will be time to seek the advice of some sober and discreet physician. In this part, I hope, I shall find an easy belief; and no body can have a pretence to doubt the advice of one who has spent some time in the study of physick, when he counsels you not to be too forward in making use of *physick* and *physicians*.

30. And thus I have done with what concerns the body and health, which reduces itself to these few and easy observable rules: plenty of *open air, exercise,* and *sleep,* plain *diet,* no *wine* or *strong drink,* and very little or no *physick,* not too warm and strait *clothing,* especially the *head* and *feet* kept cold, and the *feet* often us'd to cold water, and expos'd to wet.

Sections 31–40

31. Due care being had to keep the body in strength and vigour, so that it may be able to obey and execute the orders of the *mind;* the next and principal business is, to set the *mind* right, that on all occasions it may be dispos'd to consent to nothing but what may be suitable to the dignity and excellency of a rational creature.

32. If what I have said in the beginning of this discourse be true, as I do not doubt but it is, *viz.* That the difference to be found in the manners and abilities of men is owing more to their *education* than to any thing else, we have reason to conclude, that great care is to be had of the forming children's *minds,* and giving them that seasoning early, which shall influence their lives always after: For when they do well or ill, the praise and blame will be laid there; and when any thing is done awkwardly, the common saying will pass upon them, that it's suitable to their *breeding.*

33. As the strength of the body lies chiefly in being able to endure hardships, so also does that of the mind. And the great principle and foundation of all virtue and worth is plac'd in this: that a man is able to *deny himself* his own desires, cross his own inclinations, and purely follow what reason directs as best, tho' the appetite lean the other way.

34. The great mistake I have observ'd in people's breeding their children, has been, that this has not been taken care enough of in its *due season:* that the mind has not been made obedient to discipline, and pliant to reason, when at first it was most tender, most easy to be bow'd. Parents being wisely ordain'd by nature to love their children, are very apt, if reason watch not that natural affection very warily, are apt, I say, to let it run into fondness. They love their little ones and it is their duty; but they often, with them, cherish their faults too. They must not be cross'd, forsooth; they must be permitted to have their wills in all things; and they being in their infancies not capable of great vices, their parents think they may safe enough indulge their irregularities, and make themselves sport with that pretty perverseness which they think well enough becomes that innocent age. But to a fond parent, that would not have his child corrected for a perverse trick, but excus'd it, saying it was a small matter, *Solon* very well reply'd, *aye, but custom is a great one.*

35. The fondling must be taught to strike and call names, must have what he cries for, and do what he pleases. Thus parents, by humouring

and cockering them when *little,* corrupt the principles of nature in their children, and wonder afterwards to taste the bitter waters, when they themselves have poison'd the fountain. For when their children are grown up, and these ill habits with them; when they are now too big to be dandled, and their parents can no longer make use of them as play-things, then they complain that the brats are untoward and perverse; then they are offended to see them wilful, and are troubled with those ill humours which they themselves infus'd and fomented in them; and then, perhaps too late, would be glad to get out those weeds which their own hands have planted, and which now have taken too deep root to be easily extirpated. For he that hath been us'd to have his will in every thing, as long as he was in coats, why should we think it strange, that he should desire it, and contend for it still, when he is in breeches? Indeed, as he grows more towards a man, age shews his faults the more; so that there be few parents then so blind as not to see them, few so insensible as not to feel the ill effects of their own indulgence. He had the will of his maid before he could speak or go; he had the mastery of his parents ever since he could prattle; and why, now he is grown up, is stronger and wiser than he was then, why now of a sudden must he be restrain'd and curb'd? Why must he at seven, fourteen, or twenty years old, lose the privilege, which the parents' indulgence 'till then so largely allow'd him? Try it in a dog or an horse or any other creature, and see whether the ill and resty tricks they have learn'd when young, are easily to be mended when they are knit; and yet none of those creatures are half so wilful and proud, or half so desirous to be masters of themselves and others, as man.

36. We are generally wise enough to begin with them when they are *very young,* and discipline *betimes* those other creatures we would make useful and good for somewhat. They are only our own offspring, that we neglect in this point; and having made them ill children, we foolishly expect they should be good men. For if the child must have grapes or sugar-plums when he has a mind to them, rather than make the poor baby cry or be out of humour; why, when, he is grown up, must he not be satisfy'd too, if his desires carry him to wine or women? They are objects as suitable to the longing of one of more years, as what he cry'd for, when little, was to the inclinations of a child. The having desires accommodated to the apprehensions and relish of those several ages, is not the fault; but the not having them subject to the rules and restraints of reason: the difference lies not in having or not having appetites, but in the power to govern, and deny ourselves in them. He that is not us'd to submit his will to the reason of others *when he is young,* will scarce hearken to submit to his own reason when he is of an age to make use of it. And what kind of a man such an one is like to prove, is easy to foresee.

37. These are oversights usually committed by those who seem to take the greatest care of their children's education. But if we look into the common management of children, we shall have reason to wonder, in the great dissoluteness of manners which the world complains of, that

there are any footsteps at all left of virtue. I desire to know what vice can be nam'd, which parents, and those about children, do not season them with, and drop into 'em the seeds of, as soon as they are capable to receive them? I do not mean by the examples they give, and the patterns they set before them, which is encouragement enough; but that which I would take notice of here is, the downright teaching them vice, and actual putting them out of the way of virtue. Before they can go, they principle 'em with violence, revenge, and cruelty. *Give me a blow, that I may beat him,* is a lesson which most children every day hear; and it is thought nothing, because their hands have not strength to do any mischief. But I ask, does not this corrupt their mind? Is not this the way of force and violence, that they are set in? And if they have been taught when little, to strike and hurt others by proxy, and encourag'd to rejoice in the harm they have brought upon them, and see them suffer, are they not prepar'd to do it when they are strong enough to be felt themselves, and can strike to some purpose?

The coverings of our bodies which are for modesty, warmth and defence, are by the folly or vice of parents recommended to their children for other uses. They are made matters of vanity and emulation. A child is set a-longing after a new suit, for the finery of it; and when the little girl is trick'd up in her new gown and commode, how can her mother do less than teach her to admire herself, by calling her, *her little queen* and *her princess?* Thus the little ones are taught to be *proud* of their clothes before they can put them on. And why should they not continue to value themselves for their outside fashionableness of the taylor or tirewoman's making, when their parents have so early instructed them to do so?

Lying and equivocations, and excuses little different from lying, are put into the mouths of young people, and commended in apprentices and children, whilst they are for their master's or parents' advantage. And can it be thought, that he that finds the straining of truth dispens'd with, and encourag'd, whilst it is for his godly master's turn, will not make use of that privilege for himself, when it may be for his own profit?

Those of the meaner sort are hinder'd, by the straitness of their fortunes, from encouraging *intemperance* in their children by the temptation of their diet, or invitations to eat or drink more than enough; but their own ill examples, whenever plenty comes in their way, shew, that 'tis not the dislike of drunkenness or gluttony, that keeps them from excess, but want of materials. But if we look into the houses of those who are a little warmer in their fortunes, their eating and drinking are made so much the great business and happiness of life, that children are thought neglected, if they have not their share of it. Sauces and ragoos, and food disguis'd by all the arts of cookery, must tempt their palates, when their bellies are full; and then, for fear the stomach should be overcharg'd, a pretence is found for t'other glass of wine to help digestion, tho' it only serves to increase the surfeit.

Is my young master a little out of order, the first question is, *What will my dear eat? What shall I get for thee?* Eating and drinking are instantly press'd; and every body's invention is set on work, to find out something luscious and delicate enough to prevail over that want of appetite, which nature has wisely order'd in the beginning of distempers, as a defence against their increase; that being freed from the ordinary labour of digesting any new load in the stomach, she may be at leisure to correct and master the peccant humours.

And where children are so happy in the care of their parents, as by their prudence to be kept from the excess of their tables, to the sobriety of a plain and simple diet, yet there too they are scarce to be preserv'd from the contagion that poisons the mind; though, by a discreet management whilst they are under tuition, their healths perhaps may be pretty well secure, yet their desires must needs yield to the lessons which every where will be read to them upon this part of *epicurism.* The commendation that *eating well* has every where, cannot fail to be a successful incentive to natural appetites, and bring them quickly to the liking and expence of a fashionable table. This shall have from every one, even the reprovers of vice, the title of *living well.* And what shall sullen reason dare to say against the publick testimony? Or can it hope to be heard, if it should call that *luxury,* which is so much own'd and universally practis'd by those of the best quality?

This is now so grown a vice, and has so great supports, that I know not whether it do not put in for the name of virtue; and whether it will not be thought folly, or want of knowledge of the world, to open one's mouth against it? And truly I should suspect, that what I have here said of it, might be censur'd as a little satire out of my way, did I not mention it with this view, that it might awaken the care and watchfulness of parents in the education of their children, when they see how they are beset on every side, not only with temptations, but instructors to vice, and that, perhaps, in those they thought places of security.

I shall not dwell any longer on this subject, much less run over all the particulars that would shew what pains are us'd to corrupt children, and instil principles of vice into them: but I desire parents soberly to consider, what irregularity or vice there is which children are not visibly taught, and whether it be not their duty and wisdom to provide them other instructions.

38. It seems plain to me, that the principle of all virtue and excellency lies in a power of denying ourselves the satisfaction of our own desires, where reason does not authorize them. This power is to be got and improv'd by custom, made easy and familiar by an *early* practice. If therefore I might be heard, I would advise, that, contrary to the ordinary way, children should be us'd to submit their desires, and go without their longings, even *from their very cradles.* The first thing they should learn to know, should be, that they were not to have anything

because it pleas'd them, but because it was thought fit for them. If things suitable to their wants were supply'd to them, so that they were never suffer'd to have what they once cry'd for, they would learn to be content without it, would never, with bawling and peevishness, contend for mastery, nor be half so uneasy to themselves and others as they are, because *from the first* beginning they are not thus handled. If they were never suffer'd to obtain their desire by the impatience they express'd for it, they would no more cry for another thing, than they do for the moon.

39. I say not this, as if children were not to be indulg'd in anything, or that I expected they should in hanging-sleeves have the reason and conduct of counsellors. I consider them as children, who must be tenderly us'd, who must play, and have play-things. That which I mean, is, that whenever they crav'd what was not fit for them to have or do, they should not be permitted it because they were *little,* and desir'd it: nay, whatever they were importunate for, they should be sure, for that very reason, to be deny'd. I have seen children at a table, who, whatever was there, never ask'd for anything, but contentedly took what was given them; and at another place, I have seen others cry for everything they saw; must be serv'd out of every dish, and that first too. What made this vast difference but this? that one was accustom'd to have what they call'd or cry'd for, the other to go without it. The *younger* they are, the less I think are their unruly and disorderly appetites to be comply'd with; and the less reason they have of their own, the more are they to be under the absolute power and restraint of those in whose hands they are. From which I confess it will follow, that none but discreet people should be about them. If the world commonly does otherwise, I cannot help that. I am saying what I think should be; which if it were already in fashion, I should not need to trouble the world with a discourse on this subject. But yet I doubt not, but when it is consider'd, there will be others of opinion with me, that the *sooner* this way is begun with children, the easier it will be for them and their governors too; and that this ought to be observ'd as an inviolable maxim, that whatever once is deny'd them, they are certainly not to obtain by crying or importunity, unless one has a mind to teach them to be impatient and troublesome, by rewarding them for it when they are so.

40. Those therefore that intend ever to govern their children, should begin it whilst they are *very little,* and look that they perfectly comply with the will of their parents. Would you have your son obedient to you when past a child; be sure then to establish the authority of a father *as soon* as he is capable of submission, and can understand in whose power he is. If you would have him stand in awe of you, imprint it in his *infancy;* and as he approaches more to a man, admit him nearer to your familiarity; so shall you have him your obedient subject (as is fit) whilst he is a child, and your affectionate friend when he is a man. For methinks they mightily misplace the treatment due to their children, who are indulgent and familiar when they are little, but severe to them,

33

and keep them at a distance, when they are grown up: for liberty and indulgence can do no good to *children;* their want of judgment makes them stand in need of restraint and discipline; and on the contrary, imperiousness and severity is but an ill way of treating men, who have reason of their own to guide them; unless you have a mind to make your children, when grown up, weary of you, and secretly to say within themselves, *When will you die, father?*

Sections 41–50

41. I imagine every one will judge it reasonable, that their children, *when little,* should look upon their parents as their lords, their absolute governors, and as such stand in awe of them; and that when they come to riper years, they should look on them as their best, as their only sure friends, and as such love and reverence them. The way I have mention'd, if I mistake not, is the only one to obtain this. We must look upon our children, when grown up, to be like ourselves, with the same passions, the same desires. We would be thought rational creatures, and have our freedom; we love not to be uneasy under constant rebukes and brow-beatings, nor can we bear severe humours and great distance in those we converse with. Whoever has such treatment when he is a man, will look out other company, other friends, other conversation, with whom he can be at ease. If therefore a strict hand be kept over children *from the beginning,* they will in that age be tractable, and quietly submit to it, as never having known any other: and if, as they grow up to the use of reason, the rigour of government be, as they deserve it, gently relax'd, the father's brow more smooth'd to them, and the distance by degrees abated, his former restraints will increase their love, when they find it was only a kindness to them, and a care to make them capable to deserve the favour of their parents, and the esteem of everybody else.

42. Thus much for the settling your authority over your children in general. <u>Fear and awe ought to give you the first power over their minds, and love and friendship in riper years to hold it</u>: for the time must come, when they will be past the rod and correction; and then, if the love of you make them not obedient and dutiful, if the love of virtue and reputation keep them not in laudable courses, I ask, what hold will you have upon them to turn them to it? Indeed, fear of having a scanty portion if they displease you, may make them slaves to your estate, but they will be nevertheless ill and wicked in private; and that restraint will not last always. Every man must some time or other be trusted to himself and his own conduct; and he that is a good, a virtuous, and able man, must be made so within. And therefore what he is to receive from education, what is to sway and influence his life, must be something put into him betimes; habits woven into the very principles of his nature, and not a counterfeit carriage, and dissembled outside, put on by fear, only to avoid the present anger of a father who perhaps may disinherit him.

43. This being laid down in general, as the course that ought to be taken, 'tis fit we now come to consider the parts of the discipline to be us'd, a little more particularly. I have spoken so much of carrying a *strict hand* over children, that perhaps I shall be suspected of not considering enough, what is due to their tender age and constitutions. But that opinion will vanish, when you have heard me a little farther: for I am very apt to think, that *great severity* of punishment does but very little good, nay, great harm in education; and I believe it will be found that, *cæteris paribus,* those children who have been most *chastis'd,* seldom make the best men. All that I have hitherto contended for, is, that whatsoever *rigor* is necessary, it is more to be us'd, the younger children are; and having by a due application wrought its effect, it is to be relax'd, and chang'd into a milder sort of government.

44. A compliance and suppleness of their wills, being by a steady hand introduc'd by parents, before children have memories to retain the beginnings of it, will seem natural to them, and work afterwards in them as if it were so, preventing all occasions of struggling or repining. The only care is, that it be begun early, and inflexibly kept to 'till *awe* and *respect* be grown familiar, and there appears not the least reluctancy in the submission, and ready obedience of their minds. When this *reverence* is once thus established, (which it must be early, or else it will cost pains and blows to recover it, and the more the longer it is deferr'd) 'tis by it, still mix'd with as much indulgence as they make not an ill use of, and not by *beating, chiding,* or other *servile punishments,* they are for the future to be govern'd as they grow up to more understanding.

45. That this is so, will be easily allow'd, when it is but consider'd, what is to be aim'd at in an ingenuous education; and upon what it turns.

1. He that has not a mastery over his inclinations, he that knows not how to *resist* the importunity of *present pleasure or pain,* for the sake of what reason tells him is fit to be done, wants the true principle of virtue and industry, and is in danger never to be good for anything. This temper therefore, so contrary to unguided nature, is to be got betimes; and this habit, as the true foundation of future ability and happiness, is to be wrought into the mind as early as may be, even from the first dawnings of knowledge or apprehension in children, and so to be confirm'd in them, by all the care and ways imaginable, by those who have the oversight of their education.

46. 2. On the other side, if the *mind* be curb'd, and *humbled* too much in children; if their *spirits* be abas'd and *broken* much, by too strict an hand over them, they lose all their vigour and industry, and are in a worse state than the former. For extravagant young fellows, that have liveliness and spirit, come sometimes to be set right, and so make able and great men; but *dejected minds,* timorous and tame, and *low spirits,* are hardly ever to be rais'd, and very seldom attain to any thing. To

avoid the danger that is on either hand, is the great art; and he that has found a way how to keep up a child's spirit easy, active, and free, and yet at the same time to restrain him from many things he has a mind to, and to draw him to things that are uneasy to him; he, I say, that knows how to reconcile these seeming contradictions, has, in my opinion, got the true secret of education.

47. The usual lazy and short way by chastisement and the rod, which is the only instrument of government that tutors generally know, or ever think of, is the most unfit of any to be us'd in education, because it tends to both those mischiefs; which, as we have shewn, are the *Scylla* and *Charybdis,* which on the one hand or the other ruin all that miscarry.

48. 1. This kind of punishment contributes not at all to the mastery of our natural propensity to indulge corporal and present pleasure, and to avoid pain at any rate, but rather encourages it, and thereby strengthens that in us, which is the root from whence spring all vicious actions, and the irregularities of life. For what other motive, but of sensual pleasure and pain, does a child act by, who drudges at his book against his inclination, or abstains from eating unwholesome fruit, that he takes pleasure in, only out of fear of *whipping?* He in this only prefers the greater *corporal pleasure,* or avoids the greater *corporal pain.* And what is it, to govern his actions, and direct his conduct by such motives as these? What is it, I say, but to cherish that principle in him, which it is our business to root out and destroy? And therefore I cannot think any correction useful to a child, where the shame of suffering for having done amiss, does not work more upon him than the pain.

49. 2. This sort of correction naturally breeds an aversion to that which 'tis the tutor's business to create a liking to. How obvious is it to observe, that children come to hate things which were at first acceptable to them, when they find themselves *whipp'd,* and *chid,* and teas'd about them? And it is not to be wonder'd at in them, when grown men would not be able to be reconcil'd to any thing by such ways. Who is there that would not be disgusted with any innocent recreation, in itself indifferent to him, if he should with *blows* or ill language be *haled* to it, when he had no mind? Or be constantly so treated, for some circumstances in his application to it? This is natural to be so. Offensive circumstances ordinarily infect innocent things which they are join'd with; and the very sight of a cup wherein any one uses to take nauseous physick, turns his stomach, so that nothing will relish well out of it, tho' the cup be never so clean and well-shap'd, and of the richest materials.

50. 3. Such a sort of *slavish discipline* makes a *slavish temper.* The child submits, and dissembles obedience, whilst the fear of the rod hangs over him; but when that is remov'd, and by being out of sight, he can promise himself impunity, he gives the greater scope to his natural inclination; which by this way is not at all alter'd, but, on the contrary,

heighten'd and increas'd in him; and after such restraint, breaks out usually with the more violence; or,

Sections 51–60

51. 4. If *severity* carry'd to the highest pitch does prevail, and works a cure upon the present unruly distemper, it often brings in the room of it a worse and more dangerous disease, by breaking the mind; and then, in the place of a disorderly young fellow, you have a *low spirited moap'd* creature, who, however with his unnatural sobriety he may please silly people, who commend tame unactive children, because they make no noise, nor give them any trouble; yet at last, will probably prove as uncomfortable a thing to his friends, as he will be all his life an useless thing to himself and others.

52. Beating them, and all other sorts of slavish and corporal punishments, are not the discipline fit to be used in the education of those we would have wise, good, and ingenuous men; and therefore very rarely to be apply'd, and that only in great occasions, and cases of extremity. On the other side, to flatter children by *rewards* of things that are pleasant to them, is as carefully to be avoided. He that will give to his son *apples* or *sugar-plumbs,* or what else of this kind he is most delighted with, to make him learn his book, does but authorize his love of pleasure, and cocker up that dangerous propensity, which he ought by all means to subdue and stifle in him. You can never hope to teach him to master it, whilst you compound for the check you gave his inclination in one place, by the satisfaction you propose to it in another. To make a good, a wise, and a virtuous man, 'tis fit he should learn to cross his appetite, and deny his inclination to *riches, finery,* or *pleasing his palate,* &c. whenever his reason advises the contrary, and his duty requires it. But when you draw him to do any thing that is fit by the offer of *money,* or reward the pains of learning his book by the pleasure of a luscious morsel; when you promise him a *lace-cravat* or a *fine new suit,* upon performance of some of his little tasks; what do you by proposing these as *rewards,* but allow them to be the good things he should aim at, and thereby encourage his longing for 'em, and accustom him to place his happiness in them? Thus people, to prevail with children to be industrious about their grammar, dancing, or some other such matter, of no great moment to the happiness or usefulness of their lives, by misapply'd *rewards* and *punishments,* sacrifice their virtue, invert the order of their education, and teach them luxury, pride, or covetousness, &c. For in this way, flattering those wrong inclinations which they should restrain and suppress, they lay the foundations of those future vices, which cannot be avoided but by curbing our desires and accustoming them early to submit to reason.

53. I say not this, that I would have children kept from the conveniences or pleasures of life, that are not injurious to their health or virtue. On the contrary, I would have their lives made as pleasant and as agreeable to them as may be, in a plentiful enjoyment of whatsoever might innocently delight them; provided it be with this caution, that they have those enjoyments, only as the consequences of the state of esteem and acceptation they are in with their parents and governors; but they should never be offer'd or bestow'd on them, as the *rewards of this or that particular performance,* that they shew an aversion to, or to which they would not have apply'd themselves without that temptation.

54. But if you take away the rod on one hand, and these little encouragements which they are taken with, on the other, how then (will you say) shall children be govern'd? Remove hope and fear, and there is an end of all discipline. I grant that good and evil, *reward* and *punishment,* are the only motives to a rational creature: these are the spur and reins whereby all mankind are set on work, and guided, and therefore they are to be made use of to children too. For I advise their parents and governors always to carry this in their minds, that children are to be treated as rational creatures.

55. *Rewards,* I grant, and *punishments* must be proposed to children, if we intend to work upon them. The mistake I imagine is, that those that are generally made use of, are *ill chosen.* The pains and pleasures of the body are, I think, of ill consequence, when made the rewards and punishments whereby men would prevail on their children; for, as I said before, they serve but to increase and strengthen those inclinations, which 'tis our business to subdue and master. What principle of virtue do you lay in a child, if you will redeem his desires of one pleasure, by the proposal of another? This is but to enlarge his appetite, and instruct it to wander. If a child cries for an unwholesome and dangerous fruit, you purchase his quiet by giving him a less hurtful sweet-meat. This perhaps may preserve his health, but spoils his mind, and sets that farther out of order. For here you only change the object, but flatter still his *appetite,* and allow that must be satisfy'd, wherein, as I have shew'd, lies the root of the mischief; and till you bring him to be able to bear a denial of that satisfaction, the child may at present be quiet and orderly, but the disease is not cured. By this way of proceeding, you foment and cherish in him that which is the spring from whence all the evil flows, which will be sure on the next occasion to break out again with more violence, give him stronger longings, and you more trouble.

56. The *rewards* and *punishments* then, whereby we should keep children in order, are quite of another kind, and of that force, that when we can get them once to work, the business, I think, is done, and the difficulty is over. *Esteem* and *disgrace* are, of all others, the most powerful incentives to the mind, when once it is brought to relish them. If you can once get into children a love of credit, and an apprehension of shame and disgrace, you have put into 'em the true principle, which will

constantly work and incline them to the right. But it will be ask'd, How shall this be done?

I confess it does not at first appearance want some difficulty; but yet I think it worth our while to seek the ways (and practise them when found) to attain this, which I look on as the great secret of education.

57. *First,* children (earlier perhaps than we think) are very sensible of *praise* and commendation. They find a pleasure in being esteem'd and valu'd, especially by their parents and those whom they depend on. If therefore the father *caress and commend them when they do well, shew a cold and neglectful countenance to them upon doing ill,* and this accompany'd by a like carriage of the mother and all others that are about them, it will, in a little time, make them sensible of the difference; and this, if constantly observ'd, I doubt not but will of itself work more than threats or blows, which lose their force when once grown common, and are of no use when shame does not attend them; and therefore are to be forborne, and never to be us'd, but in the case hereafter-mention'd, when it is brought to extremity.

58. But *secondly,* to make the sense of *esteem* or *disgrace* sink the deeper, and be of the more weight, *other agreeable or disagreeable things should constantly accompany these different states;* not as particular rewards and punishments of this or that particular action, but as necessarily belonging to, and constantly attending one, who by his carriage has brought himself into a state of disgrace or commendation. By which way of treating them, children may as much as possible be brought to conceive, that those that are commended, and in esteem for doing well, will necessarily be belov'd and cherish'd by every body, and have all other good things as a consequence of it; and on the other side, when any one by miscarriage falls into disesteem, and cares not to preserve his credit, he will unavoidably fall under neglect and contempt; and in that state, the want of whatever might satisfy or delight him will follow. In this way the objects of their desires are made assisting to virtue, when a settled experience from the beginning teaches children that the things they delight in, belong to, and are to be enjoy'd by those only who are in a state of reputation. If by these means you can come once to shame them out of their faults, (for besides that, I would willingly have no punishment) and make them in love with the pleasure of being well thought on, you may turn them as you please, and they will be in love with all the ways of virtue.

59. The great difficulty here is, I imagine, from the folly and perverseness of servants, who are hardly to be hinder'd from crossing herein the design of the father and mother. Children discountenanc'd by their parents for any fault, find usually a refuge and relief in the caresses of those foolish flatterers, who thereby undo whatever the parents endeavour to establish. When the father or mother looks sowre on the child, everybody else should put on the same coldness to him, and nobody give him countenance, 'till forgiveness ask'd, and a

41

reformation of his fault has set him right again, and restor'd him to his former credit. If this were constantly observ'd, I guess there would be little need of blows or chiding: their own ease and satisfaction would quickly teach children to court commendation, and avoid doing that which they found everybody condemn'd and they were sure to suffer for, without being chid or beaten. This would teach them modesty and shame; and they would quickly come to have a natural abhorrence for that which they found made them slighted and neglected by every body. But how this inconvenience from servants is to be remedy'd, I must leave to parents' care and consideration. Only I think it of great importance; and that they are very happy who can get discreet people about their children.

60. Frequent *beating* or *chiding* is therefore carefully *to be avoided:* because this sort of correction never produces any good, farther than it serves to raise *shame* and abhorrence of the miscarriage that brought it on them. And if the greatest part of the trouble be not the sense that they have done amiss, and the apprehension that they have drawn on themselves the just displeasure of their best friends, the pain of whipping will work but an imperfect cure. It only patches up for the present, and skins it over, but reaches not to the bottom of the sore; ingenuous *shame,* and the apprehensions of displeasure, are the only true restraint. These alone ought to hold the reins, and keep the child in order. But corporal punishments must necessarily lose that effect, and wear out the sense of *shame,* where they frequently return. Shame in children has the same place that modesty has in women, which cannot be kept and often transgress'd against. And as to the apprehension of *displeasure in the parents,* that will come to be very insignificant, if the marks of that displeasure quickly cease, and a few blows fully expiate. Parents should well consider what faults in their children are weighty enough to deserve the declaration of their anger: but when their displeasure is once declar'd to a degree that carries any punishment with it, they ought not presently to lay by the severity of their brows, but to restore their children to their former grace with some difficulty, and delay a full reconciliation, 'till their conformity and more than ordinary merit, make good their amendment. If this be not so order'd, *punishment* will, by familiarity, become a mere thing of course, and lose all its influence; offending, being chastised, and then forgiven, will be thought as natural and necessary, as noon, night, and morning following one another.

Sections 61–70

61. Concerning *reputation,* I shall only remark this one thing more of it, that though it be not the true principle and measure of virtue, (for that is the knowledge of a man's duty, and the satisfaction it is to obey his maker, in following the dictates of that light God has given him, with the hopes of acceptation and reward) yet it is that which comes nearest to it: and being the testimony and applause that other people's reason, as it were by a common consent, gives to virtuous and well-order'd actions, it is the proper guide and encouragement of children, 'till they grow able to judge for themselves, and to find what is right by their own reason.

62. This consideration may direct parents how to manage themselves in reproving and commending their children. The rebukes and chiding, which their faults will sometimes make hardly to be avoided, should not only be in sober, grave, and unpassionate words, but also alone and in private: but the commendations children deserve, they should receive before others. This doubles the reward, by spreading their praise; but the backwardness parents shew in divulging their faults, will make them set a greater value on their credit themselves, and teach them to be the more careful to preserve the good opinion of others, whilst they think they have it: but when being expos'd to shame by publishing their miscarriages, they give it up for lost, that check upon them is taken off, and they will be the less careful to preserve others' good thoughts of them, the more they suspect that their reputation with them is already blemish'd.

63. But if a right course be taken with children, there will not be so much need of the application of the common rewards and punishments as we imagine, and as the general practice has establish'd. For all their innocent folly, playing and *childish actions, are to be left perfectly free and unrestrain'd,* as far as they can consist with the respect due to those that are present; and that with the greatest allowance. If these faults of their age, rather than of the children themselves, were, as they should be, left only to time and imitation and riper years to cure, children would escape a great deal of misapply'd and useless correction, which either fails to overpower the natural disposition of their childhood, and so by an ineffectual familiarity, makes correction in other necessary cases of less use; or else if it be of force to restrain the natural gaiety of that age, it serves only to spoil the temper both of body and mind. If the noise and bustle of their play prove at any time inconvenient, or unsuitable to the place or company they are in, (which can only be

where their parents are) a look or a word from the father or mother, if they have establish'd the authority they should, will be enough either to remove or quiet them for that time. But this gamesome humour, which is wisely adapted by nature to their age and temper, should rather be encourag'd to keep up their spirits, and improve their strength and health, than curb'd and restrain'd; and the chief art is to make all that they have to do, sport and play too.

64. And here give me leave to take notice of one thing I think a fault in the ordinary method of education; and that is, the charging of children's memories, upon all occasions, with *rules* and precepts, which they often do not understand, and constantly as soon forget as given. It be some action you would have done, or done otherwise, whenever they forget, or do it awkwardly, make them do it over and over again, 'till they are perfect, whereby you will get these two advantages. *First,* to see whether it be an action they can do, or is fit to be expected of them: for sometimes children are bid to do things which upon trial they are found not able to do, and had need be taught and exercis'd in before they are requir'd to do them. But it is much easier for a tutor to command than to teach. *Secondly,* another thing got by it will be this, that by repeating the same action 'till it be grown habitual in them, the performance will not depend on memory or reflection, the concomitant of prudence and age, and not of childhood, but will be natural in them. Thus bowing to a gentleman, when he salutes him, and looking in his face, when he speaks to him, is by constant use as natural to a well-bred man, as breathing; it requires no thought, no reflection. Having this way cured in your child any fault, it is cured for ever: and thus one by one you may weed them out all, and plant what habits you please.

65. I have seen parents so heap *rules* on their children, that it was impossible for the poor little ones to remember a tenth part of them, much less to observe them. However, they were either by words or blows corrected for the breach of those multiply'd and often very impertinent precepts. Whence it naturally follow'd that the children minded not what was said to them, when it was evident to them that no attention they were capable of was sufficient to preserve them from transgression, and the rebukes which follow'd it.

Let therefore your *rules* to your son be as few as possible, and rather fewer than more than seem absolutely necessary. For if you burden him with many *rules,* one of these two things must necessarily follow; that either he must be very often punish'd, which will be of ill consequence, by making punishment too frequent and familiar; or else you must let the transgressions of some of your rules go unpunish'd, whereby they will of course grow contemptible, and your authority become cheap to him. Make but few laws, but see they be well observ'd when once made. Few years require but few *laws,* and as his age increases, when one rule is by practice well establish'd, you may add another.

66. But pray remember, children are *not* to be *taught by rules* which will be always slipping out of their memories. What you think necessary for them to do, settle in them by an indispensable practice, as often as the occasion returns; and if it be possible, make occasions. This will beget *habits* in them which being once establish'd, operate of themselves easily and naturally, without the assistance of the memory. But here let me give two cautions. 1. The one is, that you keep them to the practice of what you would have grow into a habit in them, by kind words, and gentle admonitions, rather as minding them of what they forget, than by harsh rebukes and chiding, as if they were wilfully guilty. 2. Another thing you are to take care of, is, not to endeavour to settle too many *habits* at once, lest by variety you confound them, and so perfect none. When constant custom has made any one thing easy and natural to 'em, and they practise it without reflection, you may then go on to another.

This method of teaching children by a repeated *practice,* and the same action done over and over again, under the eye and direction of the tutor, 'till they have got the habit of doing it well, and not by relying on *rules* trusted to their memories, has so many advantages, which way soever we consider it, that I cannot but wonder (if ill customs could be wondered at in any thing) how it could possibly be so much neglected. I shall name one more that comes now in my way. By this method we shall see whether what is requir'd of him be adapted to his capacity, and any way suited to the child's natural genius and constitution; for that too much be consider'd in a right education. We must not hope wholly to change their original tempers, nor make the gay pensive and grave, nor the melancholy sportive, without spoiling them. God has stamp'd certain characters upon men's minds, which like their shapes, may perhaps be a little mended, but can hardly be totally alter'd and transform'd into the contrary.

He therefore that is about children should well study their natures and aptitudes, and see by often trials what turn they easily take, and what becomes them; observe what their native stock is, how it may be improv'd, and what it is fit for: he should consider what they want, whether they be capable of having it wrought into them by industry, and incorporated there by practice; and whether it be worth while to endeavour it. For in many cases, all that we can do, or should aim at, is, to make the best of what nature has given, to prevent the vices and faults to which such a constitution is most inclin'd, and give it all the advantages it is capable of. Every one's natural genius should be carry'd as far as it could; but to attempt the putting another upon him, will be but labour in vain; and what is so plaister'd on, will at best sit but untowardly, and have always hanging to it the ungracefulness of constraint and affectation.

Affectation is not, I confess, an early fault of childhood, or the product of untaught nature. It is of that sort of weeds which grow not in the wild uncultivated waste, but in garden-plots, under the negligent hand or unskilful care of a gardener. Management and instruction, and some sense of the necessity of breeding, are requisite to make any one capable of *affectation,* which endeavours to correct natural defects, and has always the laudable aim of pleasing, though it always misses it; and the more it labours to put on gracefulness, the farther it is from it. For this reason, it is the more carefully to be watch'd, because it is the proper fault of education; a perverted education indeed, but such as young people often fall into, either by their own mistake, or the ill conduct of those about them.

He that will examine wherein that gracefulness lies, which always pleases, will find it arises from that natural coherence which appears between the thing done and such a temper of mind as cannot but be approv'd of as suitable to the occasion. We cannot but be pleas'd with an humane, friendly, civil temper wherever we meet with it. A mind free, and master of itself and all its actions, not low and narrow, not haughty and insolent, not blemish'd with any great defect, is what every one is taken with. The actions which naturally flow from such a well-form'd mind, please us also, as the genuine marks of it; and being as it were natural emanations from the spirit and disposition within, cannot but be easy and unconstrain'd. This seems to me to be that beauty which shines through some men's actions, sets off all that they do, and takes all they come near; when by a constant practice, they have fashion'd their carriage, and made all those little expressions of civility and respect, which nature or custom has establish'd in conversation, so easy to themselves, that they seem not artificial or studied, but naturally to follow from a sweetness of mind and a well-turn'd disposition.

On the other side, *affectation* is an awkward and forc'd imitation of what should be genuine and easy, wanting the beauty that accompanies what is natural; because there is always a disagreement between the outward action, and the mind within, one of these two ways: 1. Either when a man would outwardly put on a disposition of mind, which then he really has not, but endeavours by a forc'd carriage to make shew of; yet so, that the constraint he is under discovers itself: and thus men affect sometimes to appear sad, merry, or kind, when in truth they are not so.

The other is, when they do not endeavour to make shew of dispositions of mind, which they have not, but to express those they have by a carriage not suited to them. And such in conversation are all constrain'd motions, actions, words, or looks, which, though design'd to shew either their respect or civility to the company, or their satisfaction and easiness in it, are not yet natural nor genuine marks of the one or the other, but rather of some defect or mistake within. Imitation of others, without discerning what is graceful in them, or what is peculiar to their characters, often makes a great part of this. But *affectation* of all kinds, whencesoever it proceeds, is always offensive; because we naturally hate whatever is counterfeit, and condemn those who have nothing better to recommend themselves by.

Plain and rough nature, left to itself, is much better than an artificial ungracefulness, and such study'd ways of being illfashion'd. The want of an accomplishment, or some defect in our behaviour, coming short of the utmost gracefulness, often escapes observation and censure. But *affectation* in any part of our carriage is lighting up a candle to our defects, and never fails to make us be taken notice of, either as wanting sense, or wanting sincerity. This governors ought the more diligently to look after, because, as I above observ'd, 'tis an acquir'd ugliness, owing to mistaken education, few being guilty of it but those who pretend to breeding, and would not be thought ignorant of what is fashionable and becoming in conversation; and, if I mistake not, it has often its rise from the lazy admonitions of those who give rules, and propose examples, without joining practice with their instructions and making their pupils repeat the action in their sight, that they may correct what is indecent or constrain'd in it, till it be perfected into an habitual and becoming easiness.

67. *Manners,* as they call it, about which children are so often perplex'd, and have so many goodly exhortations made them by their wise maids and governesses, I think, are rather to be learnt by example than rules; and then children, if kept out of ill company, will take a pride to behave themselves prettily, after the fashion of others, perceiving themselves esteem'd and commended for it. But if by a little negligence in this part, the boy should not pull off his hat, nor make legs very gracefully, a dancing-master will cure that defect, and wipe off all that plainness of nature, which the a-la-mode people call clownishness. And since nothing appears to me to give children so much becoming confidence and behaviour, and so to raise them to the conversation of those above their age, as *dancing,* I think they should be taught to dance as soon as they are capable of learning it. For tho' this consist only in outward gracefulness of motion, yet, I know not how, it gives children manly thoughts and carriage, more than any thing. But otherwise, I would not have little children much tormented about punctilio's or niceties of breeding.

Never trouble your self about those faults in them, which you know age will cure: and therefore want of well-fashion'd civility in the carriage, whilst *civility* is not wanting in the mind, (for there you must take care to plant it early) should be the parents' least care, whilst they are young. If his tender mind be fill'd with a veneration for his parents and teachers, which consists of love and esteem, and a fear to offend them: and with *respect and good will* to all people; that respect will of itself teach those ways of expressing it, which he observes most acceptable. Be sure to keep up in him the principles of good nature and kindness; make them as habitual as you can, by credit and commendation, and the good things accompanying that state: and when they have taken root in his mind, and are settled there by a continued practice, fear not, the ornaments of conversation, and the outside of fashionable manners, will come in their due time: if when they are remov'd out of their maid's care, they are put into the hands of a well-bred man to be their governor.

Whilst they are very young, any *carelessness* is to be borne with in children, that carries not with it the marks of pride or ill nature; but those, whenever they appear in any action, are to be corrected immediately by the ways above-mention'd. What I have said concerning manners, I would not have so understood, as if I meant that those who have the judgment to do it, should not gently fashion the motions and carriage of children, when they are very young. It would be of great advantage, if they had people about them from their being first able to go, that had the skill, and would take the right way to do it. That which I complain of, is the wrong course that is usually taken in this matter. Children, who were never taught any such thing as behaviour, are often (especially when strangers are present) chid for having some way or other fail'd in good manners, and have thereupon reproofs and precepts heap'd upon them, concerning putting off their hats, or making of legs, &c. Though in this, those concern'd pretend to correct the child, yet in truth, for the most part, it is but to cover their own shame; and they lay the blame on the poor little ones, sometimes passionately enough, to divert it from themselves, for fear the by-standers should impute to their want of care and skill the child's ill behaviour.

For, as for the children themselves, they are never one jot better'd by such occasional lectures. They at other times should be shewn what to do, and by reiterated actions be fashion'd beforehand into the practice of what is fit and becoming, and not told and talk'd to do upon the spot, of what they have never been accustom'd nor know how to do as they should. To hare and rate them thus at every turn, is not to teach them, but to vex and torment them to no purpose. They should be let alone, rather than chid for a fault which is none of theirs, nor is in their power to mend for speaking to. And it were much better their natural childish negligence or plainness should be left to the care of riper years, than that they should frequently have rebukes misplac'd upon them, which neither do nor can give them graceful motions. If their minds are well-dispos'd, and principled with inward civility, a great part of the roughness which sticks to the outside for want of better teaching, time and observation will rub off, as they grow up, if they are bred in good company; but if in ill, all the rules in the world, all the correction imaginable, will not be able to polish them. For you must take this for a certain truth, that let them have what instructions you will, and ever so learned lectures of breeding daily inculcated into them, that which will most influence their carriage will be the company they converse with, and the fashion of those about them. Children (nay, and men too) do most by example. We are all a sort of camelions, that still take a tincture from things near us; nor is it to be wonder'd at in children, who better understand what they see than what they hear.

68. I mention'd above one great mischief that came by servants to children, when by their flatteries they take off the edge and force of the parents' rebukes, and so lessen their authority: and here is another great inconvenience which children receive from the ill examples which they meet with amongst the meaner servants.

They are wholly, if possible, to be kept from such conversation; for the contagion of these ill precedents, both in civility and virtue, horribly infects children, as often as they come within reach of it. They frequently learn from unbred or debauch'd servants such language, untowardly tricks and vices, as otherwise they possibly would be ignorant of all their lives.

69. 'Tis a hard matter wholly to prevent this mischief. You will have very good luck, if you never have a clownish or vicious servant, and if from them your children never get any infection: but yet as much must be done towards it as can be, and the children kept as much as may be *in*[1] *the company of their parents,* and those to whose care they are committed. To this purpose, their being in their presence should be made easy to them; they should be allow'd the liberties and freedoms suitable to their ages, and not be held under unnecessary restraints, when in their parents' or governor's sight. If it be a prison to them, 'tis no wonder they should not like it. They must not be hinder'd from being children, or from playing, or doing as children, but from doing ill; all other liberty is to be allow'd them. Next, to make them in love with the *company of their parents,* they should receive all their good things there, and from their hands. The servants should be hinder'd from making court to them by giving them strong drink, wine, fruit, playthings, and other such matters, which may make them in love with their conversation.

70. Having nam'd *company,* I am almost ready to throw away my pen, and trouble you no farther on this subject: for since that does more than all precepts, rules and instructions, methinks 'tis almost wholly in vain to make a long discourse of other things, and to talk of that almost to no purpose. For you will be ready to say, what shall I do with my son? If I keep him always at home, he will be in danger to be my young master; and if I send him abroad, how is it possible to keep him from the contagion of rudeness and vice, which is every where so in fashion? In my house he will perhaps be more innocent, but more ignorant too of the world; wanting there change of company, and being us'd constantly to the same faces, he will, when he comes abroad, be a sheepish or conceited creature.

I confess both sides have their inconveniences. Being abroad, 'tis true, will make him bolder, and better able to bustle and shift among boys of his own age; and the emulation of school-fellows often puts life and

---

[1] How much the Romans thought the education of their children a business that properly belong'd to the parents themselves, see in Suetonius, August.

industry into young lads. But still you can find a school, wherein it is possible for the master to look after the manners of his scholars, and can shew as great effects of his care of forming their minds to virtue, and their carriage to good breeding, as of forming their tongues to the learned languages, you must confess, that you have a strange value for words, when preferring the languages of the antient *Greeks* and *Romans* to that which made 'em such brave men, you think it worth while to hazard your son's innocence and virtue for a little *Greek* and *Latin*. For, as for that boldness and spirit which lads get amongst their play-fellows at school, it has ordinarily such a mixture of rudeness and ill-turn'd confidence, that those misbecoming and disingenuous ways of shifting in the world must be unlearnt, and all the tincture wash'd out again, to make way for better principles, and such manners as make a truly worthy man. He that considers how diametrically opposite the skill of living well, and managing, as a man should do, his affairs in the world, is to that mal-pertness, tricking, or violence learnt amongst schoolboys, will think the faults of a privater education infinitely to be preferr'd to such improvements, and will take care to preserve his child's innocence and modesty at home, as being nearer of kin, and more in the way of those qualities which make an useful and able man. Nor does any one find, or so much as suspect, that that retirement and bashfulness which their daughters are brought up in, makes them less knowing, or less able women. Conversation, when they come into the world, soon gives them a becoming assurance; and whatsoever, beyond that, there is of rough and boisterous, may in men be very well spar'd too; for courage and steadiness, as I take it, lie not in roughness and ill breeding.

Virtue is harder to be got than a knowledge of the world; and if lost in a young man, is seldom recover'd. Sheepishness and ignorance of the world, the faults imputed to a private education, are neither the necessary consequences of being bred at home, nor if they were, are they incurable evils. Vice is the more stubborn, as well as the more dangerous evil of the two; and therefore in the first place to be fenced against. If that sheepish softness which often enervates those who are bred like fondlings at home, be carefully to be avoided, it is principally so for virtue's sake; for fear lest such a yielding temper should be too susceptible of vicious impressions, and expose the novice too easily to be corrupted. A young man before he leaves the shelter of his father's house, and the guard of a tutor, should be fortify'd with resolution, and made acquainted with men, to secure his virtues, lest he should be led into some ruinous course, or fatal precipice, before he is sufficiently acquainted with the dangers of conversation, and has steadiness enough not to yield to every temptation. Were it not for this, a young man's bashfulness and ignorance in the world, would not so much need an early care. Conversation would cure it in a great measure; or if that will not do it early enough, it is only a stronger reason for a good tutor at home. For if pains be to be taken to give him a manly air and assurance betimes, it is chiefly as a fence to his virtue when he goes into the world under his own conduct.

It is preposterous therefore to sacrifice his innocency to the attaining of confidence and some little skill of bustling for himself among others, by his conversation with ill-bred and vicious boys; when the chief use of that sturdiness, and standing upon his own legs, is only for the preservation of his virtue. For if confidence or cunning come once to mix with vice, and support his miscarriages, he is only the surer lost; and you must undo again, and strip him of that he has got from his companions, or give him up to ruin. Boys will unavoidably be taught assurance by conversation with men, when they are brought into it; and that is time enough. Modesty and submission, till then, better fits them for instruction; and therefore there needs not any great care to stock them with confidence beforehand. That which requires most time, pains, and assiduity, is, to work into them the principles and practice of virtue and good breeding. This is the seasoning they should be prepar'd with, so as not easily to be got out again. This they had need to be well provided with, for conversation, when they come into the world, will add to their knowledge and assurance, but be too apt to take from their virtue; which therefore they ought to be plentifully stor'd with, and have that tincture sunk deep into them.

How they should be fitted for conversation, and enter'd into the world, when they are ripe for it, we shall consider in another place. But how any one's being put into a mix'd herd of unruly boys, and there learning to wrangle at trap, or rook at span-farthing, fits him for civil conversation or business, I do not see. And what qualities are ordinarily to be got from such a troop of play-fellows as schools usually assemble together from parents of all kinds, that a father should so much covet, is hard to divine. I am sure, he who is able to be at the charge of a tutor at home, may there give his son a more genteel carriage, more manly thoughts, and a sense of what is worthy and becoming, with a greater proficiency in learning into the bargain, and ripen him up sooner into a man, than any at school can do. Not that I blame the schoolmaster in this, or think it to be laid to his charge. The difference is great between two or three pupils in the same house, and three or four score boys lodg'd up and down: for let the master's industry and skill be never so great, it is impossible he should have fifty or an hundred scholars under his eye, any longer than they are in the school together: Nor can it be expected, that he should instruct them successfully in any thing but their books; the forming of their minds and manners requiring a constant attention, and particular application to every single boy, which is impossible in a numerous flock, and would be wholly in vain (could he have time to study and correct every one's particular defects and wrong inclinations) when the lad was to be left to himself, or the prevailing infection of his fellows, the greatest part of the four and twenty hours.

But fathers, observing that fortune is often most successfully courted by bold and bustling men, are glad to see their sons pert and forward betimes; take it for an happy omen that they will be thriving men, and look on the tricks they play their school-fellows, or learn from them, as a proficiency in the art of living, and making their way through the world. But I must take the liberty to say, that he that lays the foundation of his son's fortune in virtue and good breeding, takes the only sure and warrantable way. And 'tis not the waggeries or cheats practis'd amongst school-boys, 'tis not their roughness one to another, nor the well-laid plots of robbing an orchard together, that make an able man; but the principles of justice, generosity, and sobriety, join'd with observation and industry, qualities which I judge school-boys do not learn much of one another. And if a young gentleman bred at home, be not taught more of them than he could learn at school, his father has made a very ill choice of a tutor. Take a boy from the top of a grammar-school, and one of the same age bred as he should be in his father's family, and bring them into good company together, and then see which of the two will have the more manly carriage, and address himself with the more becoming assurance to strangers. Here I imagine the school-boy's confidence will either fail or discredit him; and if it be such as fits him only for the conversation of boys, he were better to be without it.

Vice, if we may believe the general complaint, ripens so fast now-a-days, and runs up to seed to early in young people, that it is impossible to keep a lad from the spreading contagion, if you will venture him abroad in the herd, and trust to chance or his own inclination for the choice of his company at school. By what fate Vice has so thriven amongst us these years past, and by what hands it has been nurs'd up into so uncontroul'd a dominion, I shall leave to others to enquire. I wish that those who complain of the great decay of Christian piety and virtue every where, and of learning and acquir'd improvements in the gentry of this generation, would consider how to retrieve them in the next. This I am sure, that if the foundation of it be not laid in the education and principling of the youth, all other endeavours will be in vain. And if the innocence, sobriety, and industry of those who are coming up, be not taken care of and preserv'd, 'twill be ridiculous to expect, that those who are to succeed next on the stage, should abound in that virtue, ability, and learning, which has hitherto made *England* considerable in the world. I was going to add courage too, though it has been look'd on as the natural inheritance of *Englishmen.* What has been talk'd of some late actions at sea, of a kind unknown to our ancestors, gives me occasion to say, that debauchery sinks the courage of men; and when dissoluteness has eaten out the sense of true honour, bravery seldom stays long after it. And I think it impossible to find an instance of any nation, however renown'd for their valour, who ever kept their credit in arms, or made themselves redoubtable amongst their neighbours, after corruption had once broke through and dissolv'd the restraint of discipline, and vice was grown to such an head, that it durst shew itself barefac'd without being out of countenance.

'Tis *virtue* then, direct *virtue,* which is the hard and valuable part to be aim'd at in education, and not a forward pertness, or any little arts of shifting. All other considerations and accomplishments should give way and be postpon'd to this. This is the solid and substantial good which tutors should not only read lectures, and talk of, but the labour and art of education should furnish the mind with, and fasten there, and never cease till the young man had a true relish of it, and plac'd his strength, his glory, and his pleasure in it.

The more this advances, the easier way will be made for other accomplishments in their turns. For he that is brought to submit to virtue, will not be refractory, or resty, in any thing that becomes him; and therefore I cannot but prefer breeding of a young gentleman at home in his father's sight, under a good governour, as much the best and safest way to this great and main end of education, when it can be had, and is order'd as it should be. Gentlemen's houses are seldom without variety of company. They should use their sons to all the strange faces that come here, and engage them in conversation with men of parts and breeding, as soon as they are capable of it. And why those who live in the country should not take them with them, when they make visits of civility to their neighbours, I know not. This I am sure, a father that breeds his son at home, has the opportunity to have him more in his own company, and there give him what encouragement he thinks fit, and can keep him better from the taint of servants and the meaner sort of people, than is possible to be done abroad. But what shall be resolv'd in the case, must in great measure be left to the parents, to be determin'd by their circumstances and conveniences; only I think it the worst sort of good husbandry for a father not to strain himself a little for his son's breeding; which, let his condition be what it will, is the best portion he can leave him. But if, after all, it shall be thought by some, that the breeding at home has too little company, and that at ordinary schools, not such as it should be for a young gentleman, I think there might be ways found out to avoid the inconveniences on the one side and the other.

Sections 71–80

71. Having under consideration how great the influence of *company* is, and how prone we are all, especially children, to imitation, I must here take the liberty to mind parents of this one thing, viz. That he that will have his son have a respect for him and his orders, must himself have a great reverence for his son. *Maxima debetur pueris reverentia.* You must do nothing before him, which you would not have him imitate. If any thing escape you, which you would have pass for a fault in him, he will be sure to shelter himself under your example, and shelter himself so as that it will not be easy to come at him, to correct it in him the right way. If you punish him for what he sees you practise yourself, he will not think that severity to proceed from kindness in you, careful to amend a fault in him; but will be apt to interpret it the peevishness and arbitrary imperiousness of a father, who, without any ground for it, would deny his son the liberty and pleasures he takes himself. Or if you assume to yourself the liberty you have taken, as a privilege belonging to riper years, to which a child must not aspire, you do but add new force to your example, and recommend the action the more powerfully to him. For you must always remember, that children affect to be men earlier than is thought; and they love breeches, not for their cut or ease, but because the having them is a mark or step towards manhood. What I say of the father's carriage before his children, must extend itself to all those who have any authority over them, or for whom he would have them have any respect.

72. But to return to the business of *rewards* and *punishments.* All the actions of childishness, and unfashionable carriage, and whatever time and age will of itself be sure to reform, being (as I have said) exempt from the discipline of the rod, there will not be so much need of beating children as is generally made use of. To which if we add learning to read, write, dance, foreign language, &c. as under the same privilege, there will be but very rarely an occasion for blows or force in an ingenuous education. The right way to teach them those things, is, to give them a liking and inclination to what you suppose to them to be learn'd, and that will engage their industry and application. This I think no hard matter to do, if children be handled as they should be, and the rewards and punishments above-mention'd be carefully apply'd, and with them these few rules observ'd in the method of instructing them.

73. 1. None of the things they are to learn, should ever be made a burthen to them, or impos'd on them as a *task*. Whatever is so propos'd, presently becomes irksome; the mind takes an aversion to it,

though before it were a thing of delight or indifferency. Let a child but be order'd to whip his top at a certain time every day, whether he has or has not a mind to it; let this be but requir'd of him as a duty, wherein he must spend so many hours morning and afternoon, and see whether he will not soon be weary of any play at this rate. Is it not so with grown men? What they do chearfully of themselves, do they not presently grow sick of, and can no more endure, as soon as they find it is expected of them as a duty? Children have as much a mind to shew that they are free, that their own good actions come from themselves, that they are absolute and independent, as any of the proudest of you grown men, think of them as you please.

74. 2. As a consequence of this, they should seldom be put about doing even those things you have got an inclination in them to, but when they have a mind and *disposition* to it. He that loves reading, writing, musick, &c. finds yet in himself certain seasons wherein those things have no relish to him; and if at that time he forces himself to it, he only pothers and wearies himself to no purpose. So it is with children. This change of temper should be carefully observ'd in them, and the favourable *seasons of aptitude and inclination* be heedfully laid hold of: and if they are not often enough forward of themselves, a good disposition should be talk'd into them, before they be set upon any thing. This I think no hard matter for a discreet tutor to do, who has study'd his pupil's temper, and will be at a little pains to fill his head with suitable ideas, such as may make him in love with the present business. By this means a great deal of time and tiring would be sav'd: for a child will learn three times as much when he is *in tune,* as he will with double the time and pains when he goes awkwardly or is dragg'd unwillingly to it. If this were minded as it should, children might be permitted to weary themselves with play, and yet have time enough to learn what is suited to the capacity of each age. But no such thing is consider'd in the ordinary way of education, nor can it well be. That rough discipline of the rod is built upon other principles, has no attraction in it, regards not what humour children are in, nor looks after favourable seasons of inclination. And indeed it would be ridiculous, when compulsion and blows have rais'd an aversion in the child to his task, to expect he should freely of his own accord leave his play, and with pleasure court the occasions of learning; whereas, were matters order'd right, learning anything they should be taught might be made as much a recreation to their play, as their play is to their learning. The pains are equal on both sides. Nor is it that which troubles them; for they love to be busy, and the change and variety is that which naturally delights them. The only odds is, in that which we call play they act at liberty, and employ their pains (whereof you may observe them never sparing) freely; but what they are to learn is forc'd upon them, they are call'd, compell'd, and driven to it. This is that, that at first entrance balks and cools them; they want their liberty. Get them but to ask their tutor to teach them, as they do often their play-fellows, instead of his calling upon them to learn, and they being satisfy'd that they act as freely in this as they do in other things, they will go on with as much

pleasure in it, and it will not differ from their other sports and play. By these ways, carefully pursu'd, a child may be brought to desire to be taught any thing you have a mind he should learn. The hardest part, I confess, is with the first or eldest; but when once he is set right, it is easy by him to lead the rest whither one will.

75. Though it be past doubt, that the fittest time for children to learn any thing, is, when their *minds* are *in tune, and well dispos'd* to it; when neither flagging of spirit, nor intentness of thought upon something else, makes them awkward and averse; yet two things are to be taken care of: 1. That these seasons either not being warily observ'd, and laid hold on as often as they return, or else, not returning as often as they should, the improvement of the child be not thereby neglected, and so he be let grow into an habitual idleness, and confirm'd in this disposition: 2. That though other things are ill learn'd, when the mind is either indispos'd, or otherwise taken up; yet it is of great moment, and worth our endeavours, to teach the mind to get the mastery over itself, and to be able, upon choice, to take itself off from the hot pursuit of one thing, and set itself upon another with facility and delight, or at any time to shake off its sluggishness, and vigorously employ itself about what reason, or the advice of another shall direct. This is to be done in children, by trying them sometimes, when they are by laziness unbent, or by avocation bent another way, and endeavouring to make them buckle to the thing propos'd. If by this means the mind can get an habitual dominion over itself, lay by *ideas* or business as occasion requires, and betake itself to new and less acceptable employments without reluctancy or discomposure, it will be an advantage of more consequence than Latin or logick or most of those things children are usually requir'd to learn.

76. Children being more active and busy in that age, than in any other part of their life, and being indifferent to any thing they can do, so they may be but doing, *dancing* and *Scotch-hoppers* would be the same thing to them, were the encouragements and discouragements equal. But to things we would have them learn, the great and only discouragement I can observe, is, that they are call'd to it, 'tis *made their business,* they are *teaz'd* and *chid* about it, and do it with trembling and apprehension; or, when they come willingly to it, are kept too long at it, till they are quite tir'd: all which intrenches too much on that natural freedom they extremely affect. And it is that liberty alone which gives the true relish and delight to their ordinary play-games. Turn the tables, and you will find they will soon change their application; especially if they see the examples of others whom they esteem and think above themselves. And if the things which they observe others to do, be order'd so, that they insinuate themselves into them as the privilege of an age or condition above theirs; then ambition, and the desire still to get forward and higher, and to be like those above them, will set them on work, and make them go on with vigour and pleasure; pleasure in what they have begun by their own desire, in which way the enjoyment of their dearly beloved freedom will be no small

encouragement to them. To all which, if there be added the satisfaction of credit and reputation, I am apt to think there will need no other spur to excite their application and assiduity, as much as is necessary. I confess, there needs patience and skill, gentleness and attention, and a prudent conduct to attain this at first. But why have you a tutor, if there needed no pains? But when this is once establish'd, all the rest will follow, more easily than in any more severe and imperious discipline. And I think it no hard matter to gain this point; I am sure it will not be, where children have no ill examples set before them. The great danger therefore, I apprehend, is only from servants, and other ill-order'd children, or such other vicious or foolish people, who spoil children both by the ill pattern they set before them in their own ill manners, and by giving them together the two things they should never have at once; I mean vicious pleasures and commendation.

77. As children should very seldom be corrected by blows, so I think frequent, and especially passionate *chiding* of almost as ill consequence. It lessens the authority of the parents, and the respect of the child; for I bid you still remember, they distinguish early betwixt passion and reason: and as they cannot but have a reverence for what comes from the latter, so they quickly grow into a contempt of the former; or if it causes a present terror, yet it soon wears off, and natural inclination will easily learn to slight such scare-crows which make a noise, but are not animated by reason. Children being to be restrain'd by the parents only in vicious (which, in their tender years, are only a few) things, a look or nod only ought to correct them when they do amiss; or, if words are sometimes to be us'd, they ought to be grave, kind, and sober, representing the ill or unbecomingness of the faults, rather than a *hasty rating* of the child for it; which makes him not sufficiently distinguish, whether your dislike be not more directed to him than his fault. Passionate chiding usually carries rough and ill language with it, which has this fartser ill effect, that it teaches and justifies it in children: and the names that their parents or præceptors give them, they will not be asham'd or backward to bestow on others, having so good authority for the use of them.

78. I foresee here it will be objected to me, what then, will you have children never beaten nor chid for any fault? This will be to let loose the reins to all kind of disorder. Not so much, as is imagin'd, if a right course has been taken in the first seasoning of their minds, and implanting that awe of their parents above mentioned. For beating, by constant observation, is found to do little good, where the smart of it is all the punishment is fear'd or felt in it; for the influence of that quickly wears out, with the memory of it. But yet there is one, and but one fault, for which, I think, children should be beaten, and that is, *obstinacy* or *rebellion*. And in this too, I would have it order'd so, if it can be, that the shame of the whipping, and not the pain, should be the greatest part of the punishment. Shame of doing amiss, and deserving chastisement, is the only true restraint belonging to virtue. The smart of the rod, if shame accompanies it not, soon ceases, and is forgotten, and

will quickly by use lose its terror. I have known the children of a person of quality kept in awe by the fear of having their shoes pull'd off, as much as others by apprehensions of a rod hanging over them. Some such punishment I think better than beating; for 'tis shame of the fault, and the disgrace that attends it, that they should stand in fear of, rather than pain, if you would have them have a temper truly ingenuous. But *stubbornness,* and an *obstinate disobedience,* must be master'd with force and blows; for this there is no other remedy. Whatever particular action you bid him do, or forbear, you must be sure to see your self obey'd; no quarter in this case, no resistance: for when once it comes to be a trial of skill, a contest for mastery betwixt you, as it is if you command and he refuses, you must be sure to carry it, whatever blows it costs, if a nod or words will not prevail; unless, for ever after you intend to live in obedience to your son. A prudent and kind mother of my acquaintance, was, on such an occasion, forc'd to whip her little daughter, at her first coming home from nurse, eight times successively the same morning, before she could master her *stubbornness,* and obtain a compliance in a very easy and indifferent matter. If she had left off sooner, and stopp'd at the seventh whipping, she had spoil'd the child for ever, and, by her unprevailing blows, only confirm'd her refractoriness, very hardly afterwards to be cur'd: but wisely persisting till she had bent her mind, and suppled her will, the only end of correction and chastisement, she establish'd her authority thoroughly in the very first occasions, and had ever after a very ready compliance and obedience in all things from her daughter; for as this was the first time, so I think it was the last too she ever struck her.

The pain of the rod, *the first* occasion that requires it, continu'd and increas'd, without leaving off till it has throughly prevail'd, should first bend the mind, and settle the parent's authority; and then gravity, mix'd with kindness, should for ever after keep it.

This, if well reflected on, would make people more wary in the use of the rod and the cudgel, and keep them from being so apt to think beating the safe and universal remedy to be apply'd at random on all occasions. This is certain, however, if it does no good, it does great harm; if it reaches not the mind, and makes not the will supple, it hardens the offender; and whatever pain he has suffer'd for it, does but endear him to his beloved *stubbornness,* which has got him this time the victory, and prepares him to contest, and hope for it for the future. This I doubt not but by ill-order'd correction many have been taught to be *obstinate* and *refractory* who otherwise would have been very pliant and tractable. For if you punish a child so, as if it were only to revenge the past fault, which has rais'd your choler, what operation can this have upon his mind, which is the part to be amended? If there were no *sturdy humor* or *wilfulness* mix'd with his fault, there was nothing in it that requir'd the severity of blows. A kind or grave admonition is enough to remedy the slips of frailty, forgetfulness, or inadvertency, and is as much as they will stand in need of. But if there were a *perverseness* in the will, if it were a design'd, resolv'd disobedience, the punishment is not to be measur'd by the greatness or smallness of the matter wherein it appear'd, but by the opposition it carries, and stands in, to that respect and submission is due to the father's orders; which must always be rigorously exacted, and the blows by pauses laid on, till they reach the mind, and you perceive the signs of a true sorrow, shame, and purpose of obedience.

This, I confess, requires something more than setting children a task, and whipping them without any more a-do if it be not done, and done to our fancy. This requires care, attention, observation, and a nice study of children's tempers, and weighing their faults well, before we come to this sort of punishment. But is not that better than always to have the rod in hand as the only instrument of government? And by frequent use of it on all occasions, misapply and render inefficacious this last and useful remedy, where there is need of it? For what else can be expected, when it is promiscuously us'd upon every little slip? When a mistake in *concordance,* or a wrong *position* in verse, shall have the severity of the lash, in a well-temper'd and industrious lad, as surely as a wilful crime in an obstinate and perverse offender; how can such a way of correction be expected to do good on the mind, and set that right? Which is the only thing to be look'd after; and when set right, brings all the rest that you can desire along with it.

79. Where a *wrong bent of the will* wants not amendment, there can be no need of blows. All other faults, where the mind is rightly dispos'd, and refuses not the government and authority of the father or tutor, are but mistakes, and may often be overlook'd; or when they are taken notice of, need no other but the gentle remedies of advice, direction, and reproof, till the repeated and wilful neglect of those, shews the fault to be in the mind, and that a manifest *perverseness* of the will lies at the root of their disobedience. But whenever *obstinacy,* which is an open defiance, appears, that cannot be wink'd at or neglected, but must, in the first instance, be subdu'd and master'd; only care must be had, that we mistake not and we must be sure it is obstinacy and nothing else.

80. But since the occasions of punishment, especially beating, are as much to be avoided as may be, I think it should not be often brought to this point. If the awe I spoke of be once got, a look will be sufficient in most cases. Nor indeed should the same carriage, seriousness, or application be expected from young children as from those of riper growth. They must be permitted, as I said, the foolish and childish actions suitable to their years, without taking notice of them. Inadvertency, carelessness, and gayety, is the character of that age. I think the severity I spoke of is not to extend itself to such unseasonable restraints. Nor is that hastily to be interpreted obstinacy or wilfulness, which is the natural product of their age or temper. In such miscarriages they are to be assisted, and help'd towards an amendment, as weak people under a natural infirmity; which, though they are warn'd of, yet every relapse must not be counted a perfect neglect, and they presently treated as obstinate. Faults of frailty, as they should never be neglected,

or let pass without minding, so, unless the will mix with them, they should never be exaggerated, or very sharply reprov'd; but with a gentle hand set right, as time and age permit. By this means, children will come to see what 'tis in any miscarriage that is chiefly offensive, and so learn to avoid it. This will encourage them to keep their wills right; which is the great business, when they find that it preserves them from any great displeasure, and that in all their other failings they meet with the kind concern and help, rather than the anger and passionate reproaches of their tutor and parents. Keep them from vice and vicious dispositions, and such a kind of behaviour in general will come with every degree of their age, as is suitable to that age and the company they ordinarily converse with; and as they grow in years, they will grow in attention and application. But that your words may always carry weight and authority with them, if it shall happen, upon any occasion, that you bid him leave off the doing of any even childish things, you must be sure to carry the point, and not let him have the mastery. But yet, I say, I would have the father seldom interpose his authority and command in these cases, or in any other, but such as have a tendency to vicious habits. I think there are better ways of prevailing with them: and a gentle persuasion in reasoning, (when the first point of submission to your will is got) will most times do much better.

Sections 81–90

81. It will perhaps be wonder'd, that I mention *reasoning* with children; and yet I cannot but think that the true way of dealing with them. They understand it as early as they do language; and, if I misobserve not, they love to be treated as rational creatures, sooner than is imagin'd. 'Tis a pride should be cherish'd in them, and, as much as can be, made the greatest instrument to turn them by.

But when I talk of *reasoning,* I do not intend any other but such as is suited to the child's capacity and apprehension. No body can think a boy or three of seven years old should be argu'd with as a grown man. Long discourses, and philosophical reasonings, at best, amaze and confound, but do not instruct children. When I say, therefore, that they must be *treated as rational creatures,* I mean that you should make them sensible, by the mildness of your carriage, and the composure even in your correction of them, that what you do is reasonable in you, and useful and necessary for them; and that it is not out of *caprichio,* passion or fancy, that you command or forbid them any thing. This they are capable of understanding; and there is no virtue they should be excited to, nor fault they should be kept from, which I do not think they may be convinced of; but it must be by such *reasons* as their age and understandings are capable of, and those propos'd always *in very few and plain words.* The foundations on which several duties are built, and the fountains of right and wrong from which they spring, are not perhaps easily to be let into the minds of grown men, not us'd to abstract their thoughts from common receiv'd opinions. Much less are children capable of *reasonings* from remote principles. They cannot conceive the force of long deductions. The *reasons* that move them must be *obvious,* and level to their thoughts, and such as may (if I may so say) be felt and touch'd. But yet, if their age, temper, and inclination be consider'd, there will never want such motives as may be sufficient to convince them. If there be no other more particular, yet these will always be intelligible, and of force, to deter them from any fault fit to be taken notice of in them, (*viz.*) That it will be a discredit and disgrace to them, and displease you.

82. But of all the ways whereby children are to be instructed, and their manners formed, the plainest, easiest, and most efficacious, is, to set before their eyes the *examples* of those things you would have them do, or avoid; which, when they are pointed out to them, in the practice of persons within their knowledge, with some reflections on their beauty and unbecomingness, are of more force to draw or deter their imitation,

63

than any discourses which can be made to them. Virtues and vices can by no words be so plainly set before their understandings as the actions of other men will shew them, when you direct their observation, and bid them view this or that good or bad quality in their practice. And the beauty or uncomeliness of many things, in good and ill breeding, will be better learnt, and make deeper impressions on them, in the *examples* of others, than from any rules or instructions can be given about them.

This is a method to be us'd, not only whilst they are young, but to be continu'd even as long as they shall be under another's tuition or conduct; nay, I know not whether it be not the best way to be us'd by a father, as long as he shall think fit, on any occasion, to reform any thing he wishes mended in his son; nothing sinking so gently, and so deep, into men's minds, as *example.* And what ill they either overlook or indulge in themselves, they cannot but dislike and be asham'd of, when it is set before them in another.

83. It may be doubted, concerning *whipping,* when as the last remedy, it comes to be necessary, at what times, and by whom it should be done; whether presently upon the committing the fault, whilst it is yet fresh and hot; and whether parents themselves should beat their children. As to the first, I think it should *not* be done *presently,* lest passion mingle with it; and so, though it exceed the just proportion, yet it lose of its due weight: for even children discern when we do things in passion. But, as I said before, that has most weight with them, that appears sedately to come from their parents' reason; and they are not without this distinction. Next, if you have any discreet servant capable of it, and has the place of governing your child (for if you have a tutor, there is no doubt) I think it is best the *smart* should come immediately *from another's hand,* though by the parent's order, who should see it done; whereby the parent's authority will be preserv'd, and the child's aversion, for the pain it suffers, rather to be turn'd on the person that immediately inflicts. For I would have a *father seldom strike his child,* but upon very urgent necessity, and as the last remedy; and then perhaps it will be fit to do it so that the child should not quickly forget it.

84. But, as I said before, *beating* is the worst, and therefore the last means to be us'd in the correction of children, and that only in cases of extremity, after all gentle ways have been try'd, and prov'd unsuccessful; which, if well observ'd, there will be very seldom any need of blows. For, it not being to be imagin'd that a child will often, if ever, dispute his father's present command in any particular instance, and the father not interposing his absolute authority, in peremptory rules, concerning either childish or indifferent actions, wherein his son is to have his liberty, or concerning his learning or improvement, wherein there is no compulsion to be us'd: there remains only the prohibition of some vicious actions, wherein a child is capable of *obstinacy,* and consequently can deserve beating; and so there will be but very few occasions of that discipline to be us'd by any one who considers well and orders his child's education as it should be. For the first seven years,

what vices can a child be guilty of, but lying or some ill-natur'd tricks; the repeated commission whereof, after his father's direct command against it, shall bring him into the condemnation of *obstinacy,* and the chastisement of the rod? If any vicious inclination in him be, in the first appearance and instances of it, treated as it should be, first with your wonder, and then, if returning again, a second time discountenanc'd with the severe brow of a father, tutor, and all about him, and a treatment suitable to the state of discredit before-mention'd; and this continu'd till he be made sensible and asham'd of his fault, I imagine there will be no need of any other correction, nor ever any occasion to come to blows. The necessity of such chastisement is usually the consequence only of former indulgences or neglects: If vicious inclinations were watch'd from the beginning, and the first irregularities which they cause, corrected by those gentler ways, we should seldom have to do with more than one disorder at once; which would be easily set right without any stir or noise, and not require so harsh a discipline as beating. Thus one by one as they appear'd, they might all be weeded out, without any signs or memory that ever they had been there. But we letting their faults (by indulging and humouring our little ones) grow up, till they are sturdy and numerous, and the deformity of them makes us asham'd and uneasy, we are fain to come to the plough and the harrow; the spade and the pick-ax must go deep to come at the roots; and all the force, skill, and diligence we can use, is scarce enough to cleanse the vitiated seed-plat, overgrown with weeds, and restore us the hopes of fruits, to reward our pains in its season.

85. This course, if observ'd, will spare both father and child the trouble of repeated injunctions, and multiply'd rules of doing and forbearing. For I am of opinion, that of those actions which tend to vicious habits, (which are those alone that a father should interpose his authority and commands in) none should be forbidden children till they are found guilty of them. For such untimely prohibitions, if they do nothing worse, do at least so much towards teaching and allowing 'em, that they suppose that children may be guilty of them, who would possibly be safer in the ignorance of any such faults. And the best remedy to stop them, is, as I have said, to shew *wonder* and *amazement* at any such action as hath a vicious tendency, when it is first taken notice of in a child. For example, when he is first found in a lie, or any ill-natur'd trick, the first remedy should be, to talk to him of it as a *strange monstrous matter,* that it could not be imagin'd he would have done, and so shame him out of it.

86. It will be ('tis like) objected, that whatsoever I fancy of the tractableness of children, and the prevalency of those softer ways of shame and commendation; yet there are many who will never apply themselves to their books, and to what they ought to learn, unless they are scourg'd to it. This, I fear, is nothing but the language of ordinary schools and fashion, which have never suffer'd the other to be try'd as it should be, in places where it could be taken notice of. *Why,* else, *does the learning of* Latin *and* Greek *need the rod, when* French *and* Italian

need it not? Children learn to dance and fence without whipping; nay, Arithmetick, drawing, &c. they apply themselves well enough to without beating: which would make one suspect, that there is something strange, unnatural, and disagreeable to that Age, in the things required in grammar-schools, or in the methods us'd there, that children cannot be brought to, without the severity of the lash, and hardly with that too; or else, that it is a mistake, that those tongues could not be taught them without beating.

87. But let us suppose some so negligent or idle, that they will not be brought to learn by the gentle ways propos'd, (for we must grant, that there will be children found of all tempers,) yet it does not thence follow, that the rough discipline of the cudgel is to be us'd to all. Nor can any one be concluded unmanageable by the *milder methods* of government, till they have been *thoroughly try'd* upon him; and if they will not prevail with him to use his endeavours, and do what is in his power to do, we make no excuses for the obstinate. Blows are the proper remedies for those; but blows laid on in a way different from the ordinary. He that wilfully neglects his book, and stubbornly refuses any thing he can do, requir'd of him by his father, expressing himself in a positive serious command, should not be corrected with two or three angry lashes, for not performing his task, and the same punishment repeated again and again upon every the like default; but when it is brought to that pass, that wilfulness evidently shews itself, and makes blows necessary, I think the chastisement should be a little more sedate, and a little more severe, and the whipping (mingled with admonition between) so continu'd, till the impressions of it on the mind were found legible in the face, voice, and submission of the child, not so sensible of the smart as of the fault he has been guilty of, and melting in true sorrow under it. If such a correction as this, try'd some few times at fit distances, and carry'd to the utmost severity, with the visible displeasure of the father all the while, will not work the effect, turn the mind, and produce a future compliance, what can be hop'd from *blows,* and to what purpose should they be any more us'd? *Beating,* when you can expect no good from it, will look more like the fury of an enrag'd enemy, than the good-will of a compassionate friend; and such chastisement carries with it only provocation, without any prospect of amendment. If it be any father's misfortune to have a son thus perverse and untractable, I know not what more he can do but pray for him. But, I imagine, if a right course be taken with children from the beginning, very few will be found to be such; and when there are any such instances, they are not to be the rule for the education of those who are better natur'd, and may be manag'd with better usage.

88. If a *tutor* can be got, that, thinking himself in the father's place, charg'd with his care, and relishing these things, will at the beginning apply himself to put them in practice, he will afterwards find his work very easy; and you will, I guess, have your son in a little time a greater proficient in both learning and breeding than perhaps you imagine. But let him by no means beat him at any time without your consent and

direction; at least till you have experience of his discretion and temper. But yet, to keep up his authority with his pupil, besides concealing that he has not the power of the rod, you must be sure to use him with great respect yourself, and cause all your family to do so too: for you cannot expect your son should have any regard for one whom he sees you, or his mother, or others slight. If you think him worthy of contempt, you have chosen amiss; and if you shew any contempt of him, he will hardly escape it from your son: and whenever that happens, whatever worth he may have in himself, and abilities for this employment, they are all lost to your child, and can afterwards never be made useful to him.

89. As the father's example must teach the child respect for his tutor, so the tutor's example must lead the child into those actions he would have him do. His practice must by no means cross his precepts, unless he intend to set him wrong. It will be to no purpose for the tutor to talk of the restraint of the passions whilst any of his own are let loose; and he will in vain endeavour to reform any vice or indecency in his pupil, which he allows in himself. Ill patterns are sure to be follow'd more than good rules; and therefore he must always carefully preserve him from the influence of ill precedents, especially the most dangerous of all, the examples of the servants; from whose company he is to be kept, not by prohibitions, for that will but give him an itch after it, but by other ways I have mention'd.

90. In all the whole business of education, there is nothing like to be less hearken'd to, or harder to be well observ'd, than what I am now going to say; and that is, that children should, from their first beginning to talk, have some *discreet, sober,* nay, *wise* person about them, whose care it should be to fashion them aright, and keep them from all ill, especially the infection of bad company. I think this province requires great *sobriety, temperance, tenderness, diligence,* and *discretion;* qualities hardly to be found united in persons that are to be had for ordinary salaries, nor easily to be found any where. As to the charge of it, I think it will be the money best laid out that can be, about our children; and therefore, though it may be expensive more than is ordinary, yet it cannot be thought dear. He that at any rate procures his child a good mind, well-principled, temper'd to virtue and usefulness, and adorn'd with civility and good breeding, makes a better purchase for him that if he laid out the money for an addition of more earth to his former acres. Spare it in toys and play-games, in silk and ribbons, laces, and other useless expenses, as much as you please; but be not sparing in so necessary a part as this. 'Tis not good husbandry to make his fortune rich, and his mind poor. I have often with great admiration seen people lavish it profusely in tricking up their children in fine clothes, lodging and feeding them sumptuously, allowing them more than enough of useless servants, and yet at the same time starve their minds, and not take sufficient care to cover that which is the most shameful nakedness, *viz.* their natural wrong inclinations and ignorance. This I can look on as no other than a sacrificing to their own vanity, it shewing more their pride than true care of the good of their children;

whatsoever you employ to the advantage of your son's mind, will shew your true kindness, tho' it be to the lessening of his estate. A wise and good man can hardly want either the opinion or reality of being great and happy; but he that is foolish or vicious, can be neither great nor happy, what estate soever you leave him: and I ask you whether there be not men in the world, whom you had rather have your son be with five hundred pounds *per annum,* than some other you know with five thousand pounds.

Sections 91–100

91. The consideration of charge ought not therefore to deter those who are able. The great difficulty will be where to find a *proper person:* for those of small age, parts, and virtue, are unfit for this employment, and those that have greater, will hardly be got to undertake such a charge. You must therefore look out early, and enquire every where; for the world has people of all sorts. And I remember, *Montaigne* says in one of his essays, that the learned *Castalio* was fain to make trenchers at *Basle,* to keep himself from starving, when his father would have given any money for such a tutor for his son, and *Castalio* have willingly embrac'd such an employment upon very reasonable terms; but this was for want of intelligence.

92. If you find it difficult to meet with such a tutor as we desire, you are not to wonder. I only can say, spare no care nor cost to get such an one. All things are to be had that way: and I dare assure you, that if you can get a good one, you will never repent the charge; but will always have the satisfaction to think it the money of all other the best laid out. But be sure take no body upon friends, or charity, no, nor upon great commendations. Nay, if you will do as you ought, the reputation of a sober man, with a good stock of learning, (which is all usually requir'd in a tutor) will not be enough to serve your turn. In this choice be as curious as you would be in that of a wife for him; for you must not think of trial or changing afterwards: This will cause great inconvenience to you, and greater to your son. When I consider the scruples and cautions I here lay in your way, methinks it looks as if I advis'd you to something which I would have offer'd at, but in effect not done. But he that shall consider how much the business of a tutor, rightly employ'd, lies out of the road, and how remote it is from the thoughts of many, even of those who propose to themselves this employment, will perhaps be of my mind, that one fit to educate and form the mind of a young gentleman is not everywhere to be found, and that more than ordinary care is to be taken in the choice of him, or else you may fail of your end.

93. The character of a sober man and a scholar is, as I have above observ'd, what every one expects in a tutor. This generally is thought enough, and is all that parents commonly look for: But when such an one has empty'd out into his pupil all the Latin and logick he has brought from the university, will that furniture make him a fine gentleman? Or can it be expected, that he should be better bred, better skill'd in the world, better principled in the grounds and foundations of true virtue and generosity, than his young *tutor* is?

To form a young gentleman as he should be, 'tis fit his *governor* should himself be well-bred, understanding the ways of carriage and measures of civility in all the variety of persons, times, and places; and keep his pupil, as much as his age requires, constantly to the observation of them. This is an art not lo be learnt nor taught by books. Nothing can give it but good company and observation join'd together. The taylor may make his clothes modish, and the dancing-master give fashion to his motions; yet neither of these, tho' they set off well, make a well-bred gentleman: no, tho' he have learning to boot, which, if not well manag'd, makes him more impertinent and intolerable in conversation. Breeding is that which sets a gloss upon all his other good qualities, and renders them useful to him, in procuring him the esteem and good-will of all that he comes near. Without good breeding his other accomplishments make him pass but for proud, conceited, vain, or foolish.

Courage in an ill-bred man has the air and escapes not the opinion of brutality: Learning becomes pedantry; wit, buffoonery; plainness, rusticity; good nature, fawning. And there cannot be a good quality in him, which want of breeding will not warp and disfigure to his disadvantage. Nay, virtue and parts, though they are allow'd their due commendation, yet are not enough to procure a man a good reception, and make him welcome wherever he comes. No body contents himself with rough diamonds, and wears them so, who would appear with advantage. When they are polish'd and set, then they give a lustre. Good qualities are the substantial riches of the mind, but 'tis good breeding sets them off: and he that will be acceptable, must give beauty, as well as strength, to his actions. Solidity, or even usefulness, is not enough: a graceful way and fashion in every thing, is that which gives the ornament and liking. And in most cases, the manner of doing is of more consequence than the thing done; and upon that depends the satisfaction or disgust wherewith it is receiv'd. This therefore, which lies not in the putting off the hat, nor making of compliments, but in a due and free composure of language, looks, motion, posture, place, &c. suited to persons and occasions, and can be learn'd only by habit and use, though it be above the capacity of children, and little ones should not be perplex'd about it, yet it ought to be begun and in a good measure learn'd by a young gentleman whilst he is under a tutor, before he comes into the world upon his own legs: for then usually it is too late to hope to reform several habitual indecencies, which lie in little things. For the carriage is not as it should be, till it is become natural in every part, falling, as skilful musicians' fingers do, into harmonious order without care and without thought. If in conversation a man's mind be taken up with a solicitous watchfulness about any part of his behaviour; instead of being mended by it, it will be constrain'd, uneasy, and ungraceful.

Besides, this part is most necessary to be form'd by the hand and care of a *governor,* because, though the errors committed in breeding are the first that are taken notice of by others, yet they are the last that any one is told of; not but that the malice of the world is forward enough to tattle of them; but it is always out of his hearing, who should make profit of their judgment and reform himself by their censure. And indeed, this is so nice a point to be meddled with, that even those who are friends, and wish it were mended, scarce ever dare mention it, and tell those they love that they are guilty in such or such cases of ill breeding. Errors in other things may often with civility be shewn another; and 'tis no breach of good manners or friendship to set him right in other mistakes; but good breeding itself allows not a man to touch upon this, or to insinuate to another that he is guilty of want of breeding. Such information can come only from those who have authority over them; and from them too it comes very hardly and harshly to a grown man; and however soften'd, goes but ill down with any one who has liv'd ever so little in the world. Wherefore it is necessary that this part should be the *governor's* principal care, that an habitual gracefulness, and politeness in all his carriage, may be settled in his charge, as much as may be, before he goes out of his hands; and that he may not need advice in this point when he has neither time nor disposition to receive it, nor has any body left to give it him. The *tutor* therefore ought in the first place to be well-bred: and a young gentleman, who gets this one qualification from his *governor,* sets out with great advantage, and will find that this one accomplishment will more open his way to him, get him more friends, and carry him farther in the world, than all the hard words or real knowledge he has got from the liberal arts, or his *tutor's* learned *encyclopaedia:* not that those should be neglected, but by no means preferr'd, or suffer'd to thrust out the other.

94. Besides being well-bred, the *tutor* should know the world well; the ways, the humours, the follies, the cheats, the faults of the age he is fallen into, and particularly of the country he lives in. These he should be able to shew to his pupil, as he finds him capable; teach him skill in men, and their manners; pull off the mask which their several callings and pretences cover them with, and make his pupil discern what lies at the bottom under such appearances, that he may not, as unexperienc'd young men are apt to do if they are unwarn'd, take one thing for another, judge by the outside, and give himself up to shew, and the insinuation of a fair carriage, or an obliging application. A governor should teach his scholar to guess at and beware of the designs of men he hath to do with, neither with too much suspicion, nor too much confidence; but as the young man is by nature most inclin'd to either side, rectify him, and bend him the other way. He should accustom him to make, as much as is possible, a true judgment of men by those marks which serve best to shew what they are, and give a prospect into their inside, which often shows itself in little things, especially when they are not in parade, and upon their guard. He should acquaint him with the true state of the world, and dispose him to think no man better or worse, wiser or foolisher, than he really is. Thus, by safe and insensible degrees, he will pass from a boy to a man; which is the most hazardous

step in all the whole course of life. This therefore should be carefully watch'd, and a young man with great diligence handed over it; and not as now usually is done, be taken from a *governor's* conduct, and all at once thrown into the world under his own, not without manifest dangers of immediate spoiling; there being nothing more frequent than instances of the great looseness, extravagancy, and debauchery, which young men have run into as soon as they have been let loose from a severe and strict education: Which I think may be chiefly imputed to their wrong way of breeding, especially in this part; for having been bred up in a great ignorance of what the world truly is, and finding it a quite other thing, when they come into it, than what they were taught it should be, and so imagin'd it was, are easily persuaded, by other kind of tutors, which they are sure to meet with, that the discipline they were kept under, and the lectures read to them, were but the formalities of education and the restraints of childhood; that the freedom belonging to men is to take their swing in a full enjoyment of what was before forbidden them. They shew the young novice the world full of fashionable and glittering examples of this every where, and he is presently dazzled with them. My young master failing not to be willing to shew himself a man, as much as any of the sparks of his years, lets himself loose to all the irregularities he finds in the most debauch'd; and thus courts credit and manliness in the casting off the modesty and sobriety he has till then been kept in; and thinks it brave, at his first setting out, to signalize himself in running counter to all the rules of virtue which have been preach'd to him by his tutor.

The shewing him the world as really it is, before he comes wholly into it, is one of the best means, I think, to prevent this mischief. He should by degrees be informed of the vices in fashion, and warned of the applications and designs of those who will make it their business to corrupt him. He should be told the arts they use, and the trains they lay; and now and then have set before him the tragical or ridiculous examples of those who are ruining or ruin'd this way. The age is not like to want instances of this kind, which should be made land-marks to him, that by the disgraces, diseases, beggary, and shame of hopeful young men thus brought to ruin, he may be precaution'd, and be made see, how those join in the contempt and neglect of them that are undone, who, by pretences of friendship and respect, lead them to it, and help to prey upon them whilst they were undoing; that he may see, before he buys it by a too dear experience, that those who persuade him not to follow the sober advices he has receiv'd from his *governors,* and the counsel of his own reason, which they call being govern'd by others, do it only that they may have the government of him themselves; and make him believe, he goes like a man of himself, by his own conduct, and for his own pleasure, when in truth he is wholly as a child led by them into those vices which best serve their purposes. This is a knowledge which, upon all occasions, a *tutor* should endeavour to instil, and by all methods try to make him comprehend, and thoroughly relish.

I know it is often said, that to discover to a young man the vices of the age is to teach them him. That, I confess, is a good deal so, according as it is done; and therefore requires a discreet man of parts, who knows the world, and can judge of the temper, inclination, and weak side of his pupil. This farther is to be remember'd, that it is not possible now (as perhaps formerly it was) to keep a young gentleman from vice by a total ignorance of it, unless you will all his life mew him up in a closet, and never let him go into company. The longer he is kept thus hoodwink'd, the less he will see when he comes abroad into open daylight, and be the more expos'd to be a prey to himself and others. And an old boy, at his first appearance, with all the gravity of his ivy-bush about him, is sure to draw on him the eyes and chirping of the whole town volery; amongst which there will not be wanting some birds of prey, that will presently be on the wing for him.

The only fence against the world, is, a thorough knowledge of it, into which a young gentleman should be enter'd by degrees, as he can bear it; and the earlier the better, so he be in safe and skilful hands to guide him. The scene should be gently open'd, and his entrance made step by step, and the dangers pointed out that attend him from the several degrees, tempers, designs, and clubs of men. He should be prepar'd to be shock'd by some, and caress'd by others; warn'd who are like to oppose, who to mislead, who to undermine him, and who to serve him. He should be instructed how to know and distinguish them; where he should let them see, and when dissemble the knowledge of them and their aims and workings. And if he be too forward to venture upon his own strength and skill, the perplexity and trouble of a misadventure now and then, that reaches not his innocence, his health, or reputation, may not be an ill way to teach him more caution.

This, I confess, containing one great part of wisdom, is not the product of some superficial thoughts, or much reading; but the effect of experience and observation in a man who has liv'd in the world with his eyes open, and convers'd with men of all sorts. And therefore I think it of most value to be instill'd into a young man upon all occasions which offer themselves, that when he comes to launch into the deep himself, he may not be like one at sea without a line, compass or sea-chart; but may have some notice before-hand of the rocks and shoals, the currents and quick-sands, and know a little how to steer, that he sink not before he get experience. He that thinks not this of more moment to his son, and for which he more needs a governor, than the languages and learned sciences, forgets of how much more use it is to judge right of men, and manage his affairs wisely with them, than to speak *Greek* and *Latin,* or argue in mood and figure; or to have his head fill'd with the abstruse speculations of natural philosophy and metaphysicks; nay, than to be well vers'd in *Greek* and *Roman* writers, though that be much better for a gentleman than to be a good Peripatetick or Cartesian, because those antient authors observ'd and painted mankind well, and give the best light into that kind of knowledge. He that goes into the eastern parts of *Asia,* will find able and acceptable men without any of these; but without virtue, knowledge of the world, and civility, an accomplish'd and valuable man can be found no where.

A great part of the learning now in fashion in the schools of *Europe,* and that goes ordinarily into the round of education, a gentleman may in a good measure be unfurnish'd with, without any great disparagement to himself or prejudice to his affairs. But prudence and good breeding are in all the stations and occurrences of life necessary; and most young men suffer in the want of them, and come rawer and more awkward into the world than they should, for this very reason, because these qualities, which are of all other the most necessary to be taught, and stand most in need of the assistance and help of a teacher, are generally neglected and thought but a slight or no part of a *tutor's* business. *Latin* and learning make all the noise; and the main stress is laid upon his proficiency in things a great part whereof belong not to a gentleman's calling; which is to have the knowledge of a man of business, a carriage suitable to his rank, and to be eminent and useful in his country, according to his station. Whenever either spare hours from that, or an inclination to perfect himself in some parts of knowledge, which his *tutor* did but just enter him in, set him upon any study, the first rudiments of it, which he learn'd before, will open the way enough for his own industry to carry him as far as his fancy will prompt, or his parts enable him to go. Or, if he thinks it may save his time and pains to be help'd over some difficulties by the hand of a master, he may then take a man that is perfectly well skilled in it, or chuse such an one as he thinks fittest for his purpose. But to initiate his pupil in any part of learning, as far as is necessary for a young man in the ordinary course of his studies, an ordinary skill in the *governor* is enough. Nor is it requisite that he should be a thorough scholar, or possess in perfection all those sciences which 'tis convenient a young gentleman should have a taste of in some general view, or short system. A gentleman that would penetrate deeper must do it by his own genius and industry afterwards: For no body ever went far in knowledge, or became eminent in any of the sciences, by the discipline and constraint of a master.

The great work of a *governor,* is to fashion the carriage, and form the mind; to settle in his pupil good habits and the principles of virtue and wisdom; to give him by little and little a view of mankind, and work him into a love and imitation of what is excellent and praise-worthy; and, in the prosecution of it, to give him vigour, activity, and industry. The studies which he sets him upon, are but as it were the exercises of his faculties, and employment of his time, to keep him from sauntering and idleness, to teach him application, and accustom him to take pains, and to give him some little taste of what his own industry must perfect. For who expects, that under a *tutor* a young gentleman should be an accomplish'd critick, orator, or logician? go to the bottom of metaphysicks, natural philosophy, or mathematicks? or be a master in history or chronology? though something of each of these is to be taught him: But it is only to open the door, that he may look in, and as it were begin an acquaintance, but not to dwell there: And a *governor* would be much blam'd that should keep his pupil too long, and lead him too far in most of them. But of good breeding, knowledge of the world, virtue industry, and a love of reputation, he cannot have too much: And if he have these, he will not long want what he needs or desires of the other.

And since it cannot be hop'd he should have time and strength to learn all things, most pains should be taken about that which is most necessary; and that principally look'd after which will be of most and frequentest use to him in the world.

Seneca complains of the contrary practice in his time; and yet the *Burgursdicius's* and the *Scheiblers* did not swarm in those days as they do now in these. What would he have thought if he had liv'd now, when the *tutors* think it their great business to fill the studies and heads of their pupils with such authors as these? He would have had much more reason to say, as he does, *non vitæ sed scholæ discimus,* we learn not to live, but to dispute; and our education fits us rather for the university than the world. But 'tis no wonder if those who make the fashion suit it to what they have, and not to what their pupils want. The fashion being once establish'd, who can think it strange, that in this, as well as in all other things, it should prevail? And that the greatest part of those, who find their account in an easy submission to it, should be ready to cry out, *Heresy,* when any one departs from it? 'Tis nevertheless matter of astonishment that men of quality and parts should suffer themselves to be so far misled by custom and implicit faith. Reason, if consulted with, would advise, that their children's time should be spent in acquiring what might be useful to them when they come to be men, rather than to have their heads stuff'd with a deal of trash, a great part whereof they usually never do ('tis certain they never need to) think on again as long as they live: and so much of it as does stick by them they are only the worse for. This is so well known, that I appeal to parents themselves, who have been at cost to have their young heirs taught it, whether it be not ridiculous for their sons to have any tincture of that sort of learning, when they come abroad into the world? whether any appearance of it would not lessen and disgrace them in company? And that certainly must be an admirable acquisition, and deserves well to make a part in education, which men are asham'd of where they are most concern'd to shew their parts and breeding.

There is yet another reason why politeness of manners, and knowledge of the world should principally be look'd after in a *tutor;* and that is, because a man of parts and years may enter a lad far enough in any of those sciences, which he has no deep insight into himself. Books in these will be able to furnish him, and give him light and precedency enough to go before a young follower: but he will never be able to set another right in the knowledge of the world, and above all in breeding, who is a novice in them himself.

This is a knowledge he must have about him, worn into him by use and conversation and a long forming himself by what he has observ'd to be practis'd and allow'd in the best company. This, if he has it not of his own, is no where to be borrowed for the use of his pupil; or if he could find pertinent treatises of it in books that would reach all the particulars of an *English* gentleman's behaviour, his own ill-fashion'd example, if he be not well-bred himself, would spoil all his lectures; it being impossible, that any one should come forth well-fashion'd out of unpolish'd, ill-bred company.

I say this, not that I think such a *tutor* is every day to be met with, or to be had at the ordinary rates; but that those who are able, may not be sparing of enquiry or cost in what is of so great moment; and that other parents, whose estates will not reach to greater salaries, may yet remember what they should principally have an eye to in the choice of one to whom they would commit the education of their children; and what part they should chiefly look after themselves, whilst they are under their care, and as often as they come within their observation; and not think that all lies in *Latin* and *French* or some dry systems of logick and philosophy.

95. But to return to our method again. Though I have mention'd the severity of the father's brow, and the awe settled thereby in the mind of children when young, as one main instrument whereby their education is to be manag'd; yet I am far from being of an opinion that it should be continu'd all along to them, whilst they are under the discipline and government of pupilage; I think it should be relax'd, as fast as their age, discretion and good behaviour could allow it; even to that degree, that a father will do well, as his son grows up, and is capable of it, to *talk familiarly* with him; nay, *ask his advice, and consult* with him about those things wherein he has any knowledge or understanding. By this, the father will gain two things, both of great moment. The one is, that it will put serious considerations into his son's thoughts, better than any rules or advices he can give him. The sooner you *treat him as a man,* the sooner he will begin to be one: and if you admit him into serious discourses sometimes with you, you will insensibly raise his mind above the usual amusements of youth, and those trifling occupations which it is commonly wasted in. For it is easy to observe, that many young men continue longer in the thought and conversation of school-boys than otherwise they would, because their parents keep them at that distance, and in that low rank, by all their carriage to them.

96. Another thing of greater consequence, which you will obtain by such a way of treating him, will be *his friendship.* Many fathers, though they proportion to their sons liberal allowances, according to their age and condition, yet they keep the knowledge of their estates and concerns from them with as much reservedness as if they were guarding a secret of state from a spy or an enemy. This, if it looks not like jealousy, yet it wants those marks of kindness and intimacy which a father should shew to his son, and no doubt often hinders or abates that

chearfulness and satisfaction wherewith a son should address himself to and rely upon his father. And I cannot but often wonder to see fathers who love their sons very well, yet so order the matter by a constant stiffness and a mien of authority and distance to them all their lives, as if they were never to enjoy, or have any comfort from those they love best in the world, till they had lost them by being remov'd into another. Nothing cements and establishes friendship and good-will so much as *confident communication* of concernments and affairs. Other kindnesses, without this, leave still some doubts: but when your son sees you open your mind to him, when he finds that you interest him in your affairs, as things you are willing should in their turn come into his hands, he will be concern'd for them as for his own, wait his season with patience, and love you in the mean time, who keep him not at the distance of a stranger. This will also make him see, that the enjoyment you have, is not without care; which the more he is sensible of, the less will he envy you the possession, and the more think himself happy under the management of so favourable a friend and so careful a father. There is scarce any young man of so little thought, or so void of sense, that would not be glad of a *sure friend,* that he might have recourse to, and freely consult on occasion. The reservedness and distance that fathers keep, often deprive their sons of that refuge which would be of more advantage to them than an hundred rebukes and chidings. Would your son engage in some frolick, or take a vagary, were it not much better he should do it with, than without your knowledge? For since allowances for such things must be made to young men, the more you know of his intrigues and designs, the better will you be able to prevent great mischiefs; and by letting him see what is like to follow, take the right way of prevailing with him to avoid less inconveniences. Would you have him open his heart to you, and ask your advice? you must begin to do so with him first, and by your carriage beget that confidence.

97. But whatever he consults you about, unless it lead to some fatal and irremediable mischief, be sure you advise only as a friend of more experience; but with your advice mingle nothing of command or authority, nor more than you would to your equal or a stranger. That would be to drive him for ever from any farther demanding, or receiving advantage from your counsel. You must consider that he is a young man, and has pleasures and fancies which you are pass'd. You must not expect his inclination should be just as yours, nor that at twenty he should have the same thoughts you have at fifty. All that you can wish, is, that since youth must have some liberty, some outleaps, they might be with the ingenuity of a son, and *under the eye of a father,* and then no very great harm can come of it. The way to obtain this, as I said before, is (according as you find him capable) to talk with him about your affairs, propose matters to him *familiarly,* and ask his advice; and when he ever lights on the right, follow it as his; and if it succeed well, let him have the commendation. This will not at all lessen your authority, but increase his love and esteem of you. Whilst you keep your estate, the staff will be in your own hands; and your authority the surer, the more it is strengthen'd with *confidence* and *kindness.* For you have

not that power you ought to have over him, till he comes to be more afraid of offending so good a friend than of losing some part of his future expectation.

98. Familiarity of discourse, if it can become a father to his son, may much more be condescended to by a tutor to his pupil. All their time together should not be spent in reading of lectures, and magisterially dictating to him what he is to observe and follow. Hearing him in his turn, and using him to reason about what is propos'd, will make the rules go down the easier and sink the deeper, and will give him a liking to study and instruction: And he will then begin to value knowledge, when he sees that it enables him to discourse, and he finds the pleasure and credit of bearing a part in the conversation, and of having his reasons sometimes approv'd and hearken'd to; particularly in morality, prudence, and breeding, cases should be put to him, and his judgment ask'd. This opens the understanding better than maxims, how well soever explain'd, and settles the rules better in the memory for practice. This way lets things into the mind which stick there, and retain their evidence with them; whereas words at best are faint representations, being not so much as the true shadows of things, and are much sooner forgotten. He will better comprehend the foundations and measures of decency and justice, and have livelier, and more lasting impressions of what he ought to do, by giving his opinion on cases propos'd, and reasoning with his tutor on fit instances, than by giving a silent, negligent, sleepy audience to his tutor's lectures; and much more than by captious logical disputes, or set declamations of his own, upon any question. The one sets the thoughts upon wit and false colours, and not upon truth; the other teaches fallacy, wrangling, and opiniatry; and they are both of them things that spoil the judgment, and put a man out of the way of right and fair reasoning; and therefore carefully to be avoided by one who would improve himself, and be acceptable to others.

99. When by making your son sensible that he depends on you, and is in your power, you have established your authority; and by being inflexibly severe in your carriage to him when obstinately persisting in any ill-natur'd trick which you have forbidden, especially lying, you have imprinted on his mind that awe which is necessary; and, on the other side, when (by permitting him the full liberty due to his age, and laying no restraint in your presence to those childish actions and gaiety of carriage, which, whilst he is very young, is as necessary to him as meat or sleep) you have reconcil'd him to your company, and made him sensible of your care and love of him, by indulgence and tenderness, especially caressing him on all occasions wherein he does any thing well, and being kind to him after a thousand fashions suitable to his age, which nature teaches parents better than I can: When, I say, by these ways of tenderness and affection, which parents never want for their children, you have also planted in him a particular affection for you; he is then in the state you could desire, and you have form'd in his mind that true *reverence* which is always afterwards carefully to be continu'd,

and maintain'd in both parts of it, *love,* and *fear,* as the great principles whereby you will always have hold upon him, to turn his mind to the ways of virtue and honour.

100. When this foundation is once well lay'd, and you find this reverence begin to work in him, the next thing to be done, is carefully to consider his *temper,* and the particular constitution of his mind. Stubbornness, lying, and ill-natur'd actions, are not (as has been said) to be permitted in him from the beginning, whatever his temper be. Those seeds of vices are not to be suffer'd to take any root, but must be carefully weeded out, as soon as ever they begin to shew themselves in him; and your authority is to take place and influence his mind, from the very dawning of any knowledge in him, that it may operate as a natural principle, whereof he never perceiv'd the beginning, never knew that it was, or could be otherwise. By this, if the *reverence* he owes you be establish'd early, it will always be sacred to him, and it will be as hard for him to resist as the principles of his nature.

Sections 101–110

101. Having thus very early set up your authority, and by the gentler applications of it sham'd him out of what leads towards an immoral habit, as soon as you have observ'd it in him, (for I would by no means have chiding us'd, much less blows, till obstinacy and incorrigibleness make it absolutely necessary) it will be fit to consider which way the natural make of his *mind inclines* him. Some men by the unalterable frame of their constitutions, are *stout,* others *timorous,* some *confident,* others *modest, tractable,* or *obstinate, curious* or *careless, quick* or *slow.* There are not more differences in men's faces, and the outward lineaments of their bodies, than there are in the makes and tempers of their minds; only there is this difference, that the distinguishing characters of the face, and the lineaments of the body, grow more plain and visible with time and age; but the peculiar *physiognomy of the mind* is most discernible in children, before art and cunning have taught them to hide their deformities, and conceal their ill inclinations under a dissembled outside.

102. Begin therefore betimes nicely to observe your son's *temper;* and that, when he is under least restraint, in his play, and as he thinks out of your sight. See what are his *predominate passions* and *prevailing inclinations;* whether he be fierce or mild, bold or bashful, compassionate or cruel, open or reserv'd, &c. For as these are different in him, so are your methods to be different, and your authority must hence take measures to apply itself different ways to him. These *native propensities,* these prevalencies of constitution, are not to be cur'd by rules, or a direct contest, especially those of them that are the humbler and meaner sort, which proceed from fear, and lowness of spirit; though with art they may be much mended, and turn'd to good purposes. But this, be sure, after all is done, the byass will always hang on that side that nature first plac'd it: And if you carefully observe the characters of his mind, now in the first scenes of his life, you will ever after be able to judge which way his thoughts lean, and what he aims at even hereafter, when, as he grows up, the plot thickens, and he puts on several shapes to act it.

103. I told you before, that children love *liberty;* and therefore they should be brought to do the things are fit for them, without feeling any restraint laid upon them. I now tell you, they love something more; and that is *dominion:* And this is the first original of most vicious habits, that are ordinary and natural. This love of *power* and dominion shews itself very early, and that in these two things.

104. 1. We see children, as soon almost as they are born (I am sure long before they can speak) cry, grow peevish, sullen, and out of humour, for nothing but to have their *wills*. They would have their desires submitted to by others; they contend for a ready compliance from all about them, especially from those that stand near or beneath them in age or degree, as soon as they come to consider others with those distinctions.

105. 2. Another thing wherein they shew their love of dominion, is, their desire to have things to be theirs: They would have *propriety* and possession, pleasing themselves with the power which that seems to give, and the right they thereby have, to dispose of them as they please. He that has not observ'd these two humours working very betimes in children, has taken little notice of their actions: And he who thinks that these two roots of almost all the injustice and contention that so disturb human life, are not early to be weeded out, and contrary habits introduc'd, neglects the proper season to lay the foundations of a good and worthy man. To do this, I imagine these following things may somewhat conduce.

106. 1. That a child should never be suffer'd to have what he *craves*, much less what he *cries for*, I had said, *or so much as speaks for*: But that being apt to the misunderstood, and interpreted as if I meant a child should never speak to his parents for any thing, which will perhaps be thought to lay too great a curb on the minds of children, to the prejudice of that love and affection which should be between them and their parents; I shall explain my self a little more particularly. It is fit that they should have liberty to declare their wants to their parents, and that with all tenderness they should be hearken'd to, and supply'd, at least whilst they are very little. But 'tis one thing to say, I am hungry, another to say, I would have roastmeat. Having declar'd their wants, their natural wants, the pain they feel from hunger, thirst, cold, or any other necessity of nature, 'tis the duty of their parents and those about them to relieve them: But children must leave it to the choice and ordering of their parents, what they think properest for them, and how much; and must not be permitted to chuse for themselves, and say, I would have wine, or white-bread; the very naming of it should make them lose it.

107. That which parents should take care of here, is to distinguish between the wants of fancy, and those of nature; which *Horace* has well taught them to do in this verse:

Queis humana sibi doleat natura negatis.

Those are truly natural wants, which reason alone, without some other help, is not able to fence against, nor keep from disturbing us. The pains of sickness and hurts, hunger, thirst, and cold, want of sleep and rest or

82

relaxation of the part weary'd with labour, are what all men feel and the best dispos'd minds cannot but be sensible of their uneasiness; and therefore ought, by fit applications, to seek their removal, though not with impatience, or over great haste, upon the first approaches of them, where delay does not threaten some irreparable harm. The pains that come from the necessities of nature, are monitors to us to beware of greater mischiefs, which they are the forerunners of; and therefore they must not be wholly neglected, nor strain'd too far. But yet the more children can be inur'd to hardships of this kind, by a wise care to make them stronger in body and mind, the better it will be for them. I need not here give any caution to keep within the bounds of doing them good, and to take care, that what children are made to suffer, should neither break their spirits, nor injure their health, parents being but too apt of themselves to incline more than they should to the softer side.

But whatever compliance the necessities of nature may require, the wants of fancy children should never be gratify'd in, nor suffered to *mention*. The very *speaking* for any such thing should make them lose it. Clothes, when they need, they must have; but if they *speak* for this stuff or that colour, they should be sure to go without it. Not that I would have parents purposely cross the desires of their children in matters of indifference,; on the contrary, where their carriage deserves it, and one is sure it will not corrupt or effeminate their minds, and make them fond of trifles, I think all things should be contriv'd, as much as could be, to their satisfaction, that they may find the ease and pleasure of doing well. The best for children is that they should not place any pleasure in such things at all, nor regulate their delight by their fancies, but be indifferent to all that nature has made so. This is what their parents and teachers should chiefly aim at; but till this be obtain'd, all that I oppose here, is the liberty of *asking*, which in these things of conceit ought to be restrain'd by a constant forfeiture annex'd to it.

This may perhaps be thought a little too severe by the natural indulgence of tender parents; but yet it is no more than necessary: For since the method I propose is to banish the rod, this restraint of their tongues will be of great use to settle that awe we have elsewhere spoken of, and to keep up in them the respect and reverence due to their parents. Next, it will teach to keep in, and so master their inclinations. By this means they will be brought to learn the art of stifling their desires, as soon as they rise up in them, when they are easiest to be subdu'd. For giving vent, gives life and strength to our appetites; and he that has the confidence to turn his wishes into demands, will be but a little way from thinking he ought to obtain them. This, I am sure, every one can more easily bear a denial from himself, than from any body else. They should therefore be accustom'd betimes to consult, and make use of their reason, before they give allowance to their inclinations. 'Tis a great step towards the mastery of our desires, to give this stop to them, and shut them up in silence. This habit got by children, of staying the forwardness of their fancies, and deliberating whether it be fit or no, before they *speak,* will be of no small advantage to them in matters of greater consequence, in the future course of their lives. For that which I cannot too often inculcate, is, that whatever the matter be about which it is conversant, whether great or small, the main (I had almost said only) thing to be consider'd in every action of a child, is, what influence it will have upon his mind; what habit it tends to, and is like to settle in him; how it will become him when he is bigger; and if it be encourag'd, whither it will lead him when he is grown up.

My meaning therefore is not, that children should purposely be made uneasy. This would relish too much of inhumanity and ill-nature, and be apt to infect them with it. They should be brought to deny their appetites; and their minds, as well as bodies, be made vigorous, easy, and strong, by the custom of having their inclinations in subjection, and their bodies exercis'd with hardships: But all this, without giving them any mark or apprehension of ill-will towards them. The constant loss of what they *crav'd* or *carv'd* to themselves, should teach them modesty, submission, and a power to forbear: But the rewarding their modesty, and silence, by giving them what they lik'd, should also assure them of the love of those who rigorously exacted this obedience. The contenting themselves now in the want of what they wish'd for, is a virtue that another time should be rewarded with what is suited and acceptable to them; which should be bestow'd on them as if it were a natural consequence of their good behaviour, and not a bargain about it. But you will lose your labour, and what is more, their love and reverence too, if they can receive from others what you deny them. This is to be kept very staunch, and carefully to be watch'd. And here the servants come again my way.

108. If this be begun betimes, and they accustom themselves early to silence their desires, this useful habit will settle them; and as they come to grow up in age and discretion, they may be allow'd greater liberty, when reason comes to speak in 'em, and not passion: For whenever reason would speak, it should be hearken'd to. But as they should never be heard, when they speak for any particular thing they would *have,* unless it be first propos'd to them; so they should always be heard, and fairly and kindly answer'd, when they ask after any thing they would *know,* and desire to be inform'd about. *Curiosity* should be as carefully *cherish'd* in children, as other appetites suppress'd.

However strict an hand is to be kept upon all desires of fancy, yet there is one case wherein fancy must be permitted to speak, and be hearken'd to also. *Recreation* is as necessary as labour or food. But because there can be no *recreation* without delight, which depends not always on reason, but oftner fancy, it must be permitted children not only to divert themselves, but to do it after their own fashion, provided it be innocently, and without prejudice to their health; and therefore in this case they should not be deny'd, if they proposed any particular kind of *recreation.* Tho' I think in a well-order'd education, they will seldom be brought to the necessity of asking any such liberty. Care should be taken, that what is of advantage to them, they should always do with delight; and before they are weary'd with one, they should be timely *diverted* to some other useful employment. But if they are not yet brought to that degree of perfection, that one way of improvement can be made a recreation to them, they must be let loose to the childish play they fancy; which they should be wean'd from by being made to surfeit of it: But from things of use, that they are employ'd in, they should always be sent away with an appetite; at least be dismiss'd before they are tir'd, and grow quite sick of it, that so they may return to it again, as to a pleasure that diverts them. For you must never think them set right, till they can find delight in the practice of laudable things; and the useful exercises of the body and mind, taking their turns, make their lives and improvement pleasant in a continu'd train of *recreations,* wherein the weary'd part is constantly reliev'd and refresh'd. Whether this can be done in every temper, or whether tutors and parents will be at the pains, and have the discretion and patience to bring them to this, I know not; but that it may be done in most children, if a right course be taken to raise in them the desire of credit, esteem, and reputation, I do not at all doubt. And when they have so much true life put into them, they may freely be talk'd with about what most *delights* them, and be directed or let loose to it; so that they may perceive that they are belov'd and cherish'd, and that those under whose tuition they are, are not enemies to their satisfaction. Such a management will make them in love with the hand that directs them, and the virtue they are directed to.

This farther advantage may be made by a free liberty permitted them in their *recreations,* that it will discover their natural tempers, shew their inclinations and aptitudes, and thereby direct wise parents in the choice both of the course of life and employment they shall design them for, and of fit remedies, in the mean time, to be apply'd to whatever bent of nature they may observe most likely to mislead any of their children.

109. 2. Children who live together, often strive for mastery, whose wills shall carry it over the rest: whoever begins the *contest,* should be sure to be cross'd in it. But not only that, but they should be taught to have all the *deference, complaisance,* and *civility* one for the other imaginable. This, when they see it procures them respect, love and esteem, and that they lose no superiority by it, they will take more pleasure in, than in insolent domineering; for so plainly is the other.

The accusations of children one against another, which usually are but the clamours of anger and revenge desiring aid, should not be favourably received, nor hearken'd to. It weakens and effeminates their minds to suffer them to *complain;* and if they endure sometimes crossing or pain from others without being permitted to think it strange or intolerable, it will do them no harm to learn sufferance, and harden them early. But though you give no countenance to the *complaints* of the *querulous,* yet take care to curb the insolence and ill nature of the injurious. When you observe it yourself, reprove it before the injur'd party: but if the *complaint* be of something really worth your notice, and prevention another time, then reprove the offender by himself alone, out of sight of him that complain'd and make him go and ask pardon, and make reparation: which coming thus, as it were from himself, will be the more chearfully performed, and more kindly receiv'd, the love strengthen'd between them, and a custom of civility grow familiar amongst your children.

110. 3. As to the having and possessing of things, teach them to part with what they have, easily and freely to their friends, and let them find by experience that the most *liberal* has always the most plenty, with esteem and commendation to boot, and they will quickly learn to practise it. This I imagine, will make brothers and sisters kinder and civiller to one another, and consequently to others, than twenty rules about good manners, with which children are ordinarily perplex'd and cumber'd. Covetousness, and the desire of having in our possession, and under our dominion, more than we have need of, being the root of all evil, should be early and carefully weeded out, and the contrary quality of a readiness to impart to others, implanted. This should be encourag'd by great commendation and credit, and constantly taking care that he loses nothing by his *liberality.* Let all the instances he gives of such freeness be always repay'd, and with interest; and let him sensibly perceive, that the kindness he shews to others, is no ill husbandry for himself; but that it brings a return of kindness both from those that receive it, and those who look on. Make this a contest among children, who shall out-do one another this way: and by this means, by a constant practice, children having made it easy to themselves to part with what they have, good nature may be settled in them into an habit, and they may take pleasure, and pique themselves in being *kind, liberal and civil,* to others.

If liberality ought to be encourag'd certainly great care is to be taken that children transgress not the rules of *Justice:* and whenever they do, they should be set right, and if there be occasion for it, severely rebuk'd.

Our first actions being guided more by self-love than reason or reflection, 'tis no wonder that in children they should be very apt to deviate from the just measures of right and wrong; which are in the mind the result of improv'd reason and serious meditation. This the more they are apt to mistake, the more careful guard ought to be kept over them; and every the least slip in this great social virtue taken notice of, and rectify'd; and that in things of the least weight and moment, both to instruct their ignorance, and prevent ill habits; which from small beginnings in pins and cherry-stones, will, if let alone, grow up to higher frauds, and be in danger to end at last in downright harden'd dishonesty. The first tendency to any *injustice* that appears, must be suppress'd with a shew of wonder and abhorrence in the parents and governors. But because children cannot well comprehend what *injustice* is, till they understand property, and how particular persons come by it, the safest way to secure *honesty,* is to lay the foundations of it early in liberality, and an easiness to part with to others whatever they have or like themselves. This may be taught them early, before they have language and understanding enough to form distinct notions of property, and to know what is theirs by a peculiar right exclusive of others. And since children seldom have any thing but by gift, and that for the most part from their parents, they may be at first taught not to take or keep any thing but what is given them by those, whom they take to have power over it. And as their capacities enlarge, other rules and cases of *justice,* and rights concerning *Meum* and *Tuum,* may be propos'd and inculcated. If any act of *injustice* in them appears to proceed, not from mistake, but a perverseness in their wills, when a gentle rebuke and shame will not reform this irregular and covetous inclination, rougher remedies must be apply'd: And 'tis but for the father and tutor to take and keep from them something that they value and think their own, or order somebody else to do it; and by such instances, make them sensible what little advantage they are like to make by possessing themselves *unjustly* of what is another's, whilst there are in the world stronger and more men than they. But if an ingenuous detestation of this shameful vice be but carefully and early instill'd into 'em, as I think it may, that is the true and genuine method to obviate this crime, and will be a better guard against dishonesty than any considerations drawn from interest; habits working more constantly, and with greater facility, than reason, which, when we have most need of it, is seldom fairly consulted, and more rarely obey'd.

Sections 111–120

111. *Crying* is a fault that should not be tolerated in children; not only for the unpleasant and unbecoming noise it fills the house with, but for more considerable reasons, in reference to the children themselves; which is to be our aim in education.

Their *crying* is of two sorts; either *stubborn* and *domineering*, or *querulous* and *whining*.

1. Their *crying* is very often a striving for mastery, and an open declaration of their insolence or obstinacy; when they have not the power to obtain their desire, they will, by their *clamour* and *sobbing*, maintain their title and right to it. This is an avow'd continuing their claim, and a sort of remonstrance against the oppression and injustice of those who deny them what they have a mind to.

112. 2. Sometimes their *crying* is the effect of pain, or true sorrow, and a *bemoaning* themselves under it.

These two, if carefully observ'd, may, by the mien, looks, actions, and particularly by the tone of their crying be easily distinguished; but neither of them must be suffer'd, much less encourag'd.

1. The obstinate or *stomachful crying* should by no means be permitted, because it is but another way of flattering their desires, and encouraging those passions which 'tis our main business to subdue: and if it be, as often it is, upon the receiving any correction, it quite defeats all the good effects of it; for any chastisement which leaves them in this declar'd opposition, only serves to make them worse. The restraints and punishments laid on children are all misapply'd and lost, as far as they do not prevail over their wills, teach them to submit their passions, and make their minds supple and pliant to what their parents' reason advises them now, and so prepare them to obey what their own reason shall advise hereafter. But if in any thing wherein they are cross'd, they may be suffer'd to go away crying, they confirm themselves in their desires, and cherish the ill humour, with a declaration of their right, and a resolution to satisfy their inclination the first opportunity. This therefore is another argument against the frequent use of blows: for, whenever you come to that extremity, 'tis not enough to whip or beat them, you must do it, till you find you have subdu'd their minds, till with submission and patience they yield to the correction; which you shall best discover by their *crying*, and their ceasing from it upon your

bidding. Without this, the beating of children is but a passionate tyranny over them; and it is mere cruelty, and not correction, to put their bodies in pain, without doing their minds any good. As this gives us a reason why children should seldom be corrected, so it also prevents their being so. For if, whenever they are chastis'd, it were done thus without passion, soberly, and yet effectually too, laying on the blows and smart not furiously, and all at once, but slowly, with reasoning between, and with observation how it wrought, stopping when it had made them pliant, penitent and yielding; they would seldom need the like punishment again, being made careful to avoid the fault that deserv'd it. Besides, by this means, as the punishment would not be lost for being too little, and not effectual, so it would be kept from being too much, if we gave off as soon as we perceiv'd that it reach'd the mind, and that was better'd. For since the chiding or beating of children should be always the least that possibly may be, that which is laid on in the heat of anger, seldom observes that measure, but is commonly more than it should be, though it prove less than enough.

113. 2. Many children are apt to *cry,* upon any little pain they suffer, and the least harm that befalls them puts them into *complaints* and *bawling.* This few children avoid: for it being the first and natural way to declare their sufferings or wants, before they can speak, the compassion that is thought due to that tender age foolishly encourages, and continues it in them long after they can speak. 'Tis the duty, I confess, of those about children, to compassionate them, whenever they suffer any hurt; but not to shew it in pitying them. Help and ease them the best you can, but by no means bemoan them. This softens their minds, and makes them yield to the little harms that happen to them; whereby they sink deeper into that part which alone feels, and makes larger wounds there, than otherwise they would. They should be harden'd against all sufferings, especially of the body, and have no tenderness but what rises from an ingenuous shame, and a quick sense of reputation. The many inconveniences this life is expos'd to, require we should not be too sensible of every little hurt. What our minds yield not to, makes but a slight impression, and does us but very little harm. 'Tis the suffering of our spirits that gives and continues the pain. This brawniness and insensibility of mind, is the best armour we can have against the common evils and accidents of life; and being a temper that is to be got by exercise and custom, more than any other way, the practice of it should be begun betimes; and happy is he that is taught it early. That effeminacy of spirit, which is to be prevented or cured, as nothing that I know so much increases in children as *crying;* so nothing, on the other side, so much checks and restrains, as their being hinder'd from that sort of *complaining.* In the little harms they suffer from knocks and falls, they should not be pitied for falling, but bid do so again; which besides that it stops their *crying,* is a better way to cure their heedlessness, and prevent their tumbling another time, than either chiding or bemoaning them. But, let the hurts they receive be what they will, stop their *crying,* and that will give them more quiet and ease at present, and harden them for the future.

114. The former sort of *crying* requires severity to silence it; and where a look, or a positive command will not do it, blows must: for it proceeding from pride, obstinacy, and stomach, the will, where the fault lies, must be bent, and made to comply, by a rigour sufficient to master it. But this latter being ordinarily from softness of mind, a quite contrary cause, ought to be treated with a gentler hand. Persuasion, or diverting the thoughts another way, or laughing at their *whining,* may perhaps be at first the proper method: but for this, the circumstances of the thing, and the particular temper of the child, must be considered. No certain unvariable rules can be given about it; but it must be left to the prudence of the parents or tutor. But this, I think, I may say in general, that there should be a constant discountenancing of this sort of *crying* also; and that the father, by his authority, should always stop it, mixing a greater degree of roughness in his looks or words, proportionately as the child is of a greater age, or a sturdier temper: But always let it be enough to silence their *whimpering,* and put an end to the disorder.

115. *Cowardice* and *courage* are so nearly related to the foremention'd tempers, that it may not be amiss here to take notice of them. Fear is a passion that, if rightly governed, has its use. And though self-love seldom fails to keep it watchful and high enough in us, yet there may be an excess on the daring side; *fool-hardiness* and insensibility of danger being as little reasonable, as trembling and shrinking at the approach of every little evil. Fear was given us as a monitor to quicken our industry, and keep us upon our guard against the approaches of evil; and therefore to have no apprehension of mischief at hand, not to make a just estimate of the danger, but heedlessly to run into it, be the hazard what it will, without considering of what use or consequence it may be, is not the resolution of a rational creature, but brutish fury. Those who have children of this temper, have nothing to do, but a little to awaken their reason, which self-preservation will quickly dispose them to hearken to, unless (which is usually the case) some other passion hurries them on head-long, without sense and without consideration. A dislike of evil is so natural to mankind, that nobody, I think, can be without fear of it: fear being nothing but an uneasiness under the apprehension of that coming upon us, which we dislike. And therefore, whenever any one runs into danger, we may say, 'tis under the conduct of ignorance, or the command of some more imperious passion, nobody being so much an enemy to himself, as to come within the reach of evil, out of free choice, and court danger for danger's sake. If it be therefore pride, vain-glory, or rage, that silences a child's fear, or makes him not hearken to its advice, those are by fit means to be abated, that a little consideration may allay his heat, and make him bethink himself, whether this attempt be worth the venture. But this being a fault that children are not so often guilty of, I shall not be more particular in its cure. Weakness of spirit is the more common defect, and therefore will require the greater care.

Fortitude is the guard and support of the other virtues; and without courage a man will scarce keep steady to his duty, and fill up the character of a truly worthy man.

Courage, that makes us bear up against dangers that we fear and evils that we feel, is of great use in an estate, as ours is in this life, expos'd to assaults on all hands: and therefore it is very advisable to get children into this armour as early as we can. Natural temper, I confess, does here a great deal: but even where that is defective, and the heart is in itself weak and timorous, it may, by a right management, be brought to a better resolution. What is to be done to prevent breaking children's spirits by frightful apprehensions instill'd into them when young, or bemoaning themselves under every little suffering, I have already taken notice; how to harden their tempers, and raise their *courage,* if we find them too much subject to fear, is farther to be consider'd.

True fortitude, I take to be the quiet possession of a man's self, and an undisturb'd doing his duty, whatever evil besets, or danger lies in his way. This there are so few men attain to, that we are not to expect it from children. But yet something may be done: and a wise conduct by insensible degrees may carry them farther than one expects.

The neglect of this great care of them, whilst they are young, is the reason, perhaps, why there are so few that have this virtue in its full latitude when they are men. I should not say this in a nation so naturally brave, as ours is, did I think that true fortitude required nothing but courage in the field, and a contempt of life in the face of an enemy. This, I confess, is not the least part of it, nor can be denied the laurels and honours always justly due to the valour of those who venture their lives for their country. But yet this is not all. Dangers attack us in other places besides the field of battle; and though death be the king of terrors, yet pain, disgrace and poverty, have frightful looks, able to discompose most men whom they seem ready to seize on: and there are those who contemn some of these, and yet are heartily frighted with the other. True fortitude is prepar'd for dangers of all kinds, and unmoved, whatsoever evil it be that threatens. I do not mean unmoved with any fear at all. Where danger shews it self, apprehension cannot, without stupidity, be wanting; where danger is, sense of danger should be; and so much fear as should keep us awake, and excite our attention, industry, and vigour; but not disturb the calm use of our reason, nor hinder the execution of what that dictates.

The first step to get this noble and manly steadiness, is, what I have above mentioned, carefully to keep children from frights of all kinds, when they are young. Let not any fearful apprehensions be talk'd into them, nor terrible objects surprise them. This often so shatters and discomposes the spirits, that they never recover it again; but during their whole life, upon the first suggestion or appearance of any terrifying idea, are scatter'd and confounded; the body is enervated, and the mind disturb'd, and the man scarce himself, or capable of any composed or rational action. Whether this be from an habitual motion of the animal spirits, introduc'd by the first strong impression, or from the alteration of the constitution by some more unaccountable way, this is certain, that so it is. Instances of such who in a weak timorous mind, have borne, all their whole lives through, the effects of a fright when they were young, are every where to be seen, and therefore as much as may be to be prevented.

The next thing is by gentle degrees to accustom children to those things they are too much afraid of. But here great caution is to be used, that you do not make too much haste, nor attempt this cure too early, for fear lest you increase the mischief instead of remedying it. Little ones in arms may be easily kept out of the way of terrifying objects, and till they can talk and understand what is said to them, are scarce capable of that reasoning and discourse which should be used to let them know there is no harm in those frightful objects, which we would make them familiar with, and do, to that purpose by gentle degrees bring nearer and nearer to them. And therefore 'tis seldom there is need of any application to them of this kind, till after they can run about and talk. But yet, if it should happen that infants should have taken offence at any thing which cannot be easily kept out of their way, and that they shew marks of terror as often as it comes in sight; all the allays of fright, by diverting their thoughts, or mixing pleasant and agreeable appearances with it, must be used, till it be grown familiar and inoffensive to them.

I think we may observe, that, when children are first born, all objects of sight that do not hurt the eyes, are indifferent to them; and they are no more afraid of a blackamoor or a lion, than of their nurse or a cat. What is it then, that afterwards, in certain mixtures of shape and colour, comes to affright them? Nothing but the apprehensions of harm that accompanies those things. Did a child suck every day a new nurse, I make account it would be no more affrighted with the change of faces at six months old, than at sixty. The reason then why it will not come to a stranger, is, because having been accustomed to receive its food and kind usage only from one or two that are about it, the child apprehends, by coming into the arms of a stranger, the being taken from what delights and feeds it and every moment supplies its wants, which it often feels, and therefore fears when the nurse is away.

The only thing we naturally are afraid of is pain, or loss of pleasure. And because these are not annexed to any shape, colour, or size of visible objects, we are frighted with none of them, till either we have felt pain from them, or have notions put into us that they will do us harm. The pleasant brightness and lustre of flame and fire so delights children, that at first they always desire to be handling of it: but when constant experience has convinced them, by the exquisite pain it has put them to, how cruel and unmerciful it is, they are afraid to touch it, and carefully avoid it. This being the ground of fear, 'tis not hard to find whence it arises, and how it is to be cured in all mistaken objects of terror. And when the mind is confirm'd against them, and has got a mastery over it self and its usual fears in lighter occasions, it is in good preparation to meet more real dangers. Your child shrieks, and runs away at the sight of a frog; let another catch it, and lay it down at a good distance from him: at first accustom him to look upon it; when he can do that, then to come nearer to it, and see it leap without emotion; then to touch it lightly, when it is held fast in another's hand; and so on, till he can come to handle it as confidently as a butterfly or a sparrow. By the same way any other vain terrors may be remov'd; if care be taken, that you go not too fast, and push not the child on to a new degree of assurance, till he be thoroughly confirm'd in the former. And thus the young soldier is to be train'd on to the warfare of life; wherein care is to be taken, that more things be not represented as dangerous than really are so; and then, that whatever you observe him to be more frighted at than he should, you be sure to tole him on to by insensible degrees, till he at last, quitting his fears, masters the difficulty, and comes off with applause. Successes of this kind, often repeated, will make him find, that evils are not always so certain or so great as our fears represent them; and that the way to avoid them, is not to run away, or be discompos'd, dejected, and deterr'd by fear, where either our credit or duty requires us to go on.

But since the great foundation of fear in children is pain, the way to harden and fortify children against fear and danger is to accustom them to suffer pain. This 'tis possible will be thought, by kind parents, a very unnatural thing towards their children; and by most, unreasonable, to endeavour to reconcile any one to the sense of pain, by bringing it upon him. 'Twill be said: 'It may perhaps give the child an aversion for him that makes him suffer; but can never recommend to him suffering itself. This is a strange method. You will not have children whipp'd and punish'd for their faults, but you would have them tormented for doing well, or for tormenting sake.' I doubt not but such objections as these will be made, and I shall be thought inconsistent with my self, or fantastical, in proposing it. I confess, it is a thing to be managed with great discretion, and therefore it falls not out amiss, that it will not be receiv'd or relish'd, but by those who consider well, and look into the reason of things. I would not have children much beaten for their faults, because I would not have them think bodily pain the greatest punishment: and I would have them, when they do well, be sometimes put in pain, for the same reason, that they might be accustom'd to bear it, without looking on it as the greatest evil. How much education may reconcile young people to pain and sufference, the examples of Sparta do sufficiently shew: and they who have once brought themselves not to think bodily pain the greatest of evils, or that which they ought to stand most in fear of, have made no small advance towards virtue. But I am not so foolish to propose the *Lacedæmonian* discipline in our age or constitution. But yet I do say, that inuring children gently to suffer some degrees of pain without shrinking, is a way to gain firmness to their minds, and lay a foundation for courage and resolution in the future part of their lives.

Not to bemoan them, or permit them to bemoan themselves, on every little pain they suffer, is the first step to be made. But of this I have spoken elsewhere.

The next thing is, sometimes designedly to put them in pain: but care must be taken that this be done when the child is in good humour, and satisfied of the good-will and kindness of him that hurts him, at the time that he does it. There must no marks of anger or displeasure on the one side, nor compassion or repenting on the other, go along with it: and it must be sure to be no more than the child can bear without repining or taking it amiss, or for a punishment. Managed by these degrees, and with such circumstances, I have seen a child run away laughing with good smart blows of a wand on his back, who would have cried for an unkind word, and have been very sensible of the chastisement of a cold look, from the same person. Satisfy a child by a constant course of your care and kindness, that you perfectly love him, and he may by degrees be accustom'd to bear very painful and rough usage from you, without flinching or complaining: and this we see children do every day in play one with another. The softer you find your child is, the more you are to seek occasions, at fit times, thus to harden him. The great art in this is, to begin with what is but very little painful, and to proceed by insensible degrees, when you are playing, and in good humour with him, and speaking well of him: and when you have once got him to think himself made amends for his suffering by the praise is given him for his courage; when he can take a pride in giving such marks of his manliness, and can prefer the reputation of being brave and stout, to the avoiding a little pain, or the shrinking under it; you need not despair in time and by the assistance of his growing reason, to master his timorousness, and mend the weakness of his constitution. As he grows bigger, he is to be set upon bolder attempts than his natural temper carries him to; and whenever he is observ'd to flinch from what one has reason to think he would come off well in, if he had but courage to undertake, *that* he should be assisted in at first, and by degrees sham'd to, till at last practice has given more assurance, and with it a mastery; which must be rewarded with great praise, and the good opinion of others, for his performance. When by these steps he has got resolution enough not to be deterr'd from what he ought to do, by the apprehension of danger; when fear does not, in sudden or hazardous occurrences, discompose his mind, set his body a-trembling, and make him unfit for action, or run away from it, he has then the courage of a rational creature: and such an hardiness we should endeavour by custom and use to bring children to, as proper occasions come in our way.

116. One thing I have frequently observ'd in children, that when they have got possession of any poor creature, they are apt to use it ill: they often *torment,* and treat very roughly, young birds, butterflies, and such

other poor animals which fall into their hands, and that with a seeming kind of pleasure. This I think should be watched in them, and if they incline to any such cruelty, they should be taught to contrary usage. For the custom of tormenting and killing of beasts, will, by degrees, harden their minds even towards men; and they who delight in the suffering and destruction of inferior creatures, will not be apt to be very compassionate or benign to those of their own kind. Our practice takes notice of this in the exclusion of *butchers* from juries of life and death. Children should from the beginning be bred up in an abhorrence of *killing* or tormenting any living creature; and be taught not to *spoil* or destroy any thing, unless it be for the preservation or advantage of some other that is nobler. And truly, if the preservation of all mankind, as much as in him lies, were every one's persuasion, as indeed it is every one's duty, and the true principle to regulate our religion, politics and morality by, the world would be much quieter, and better natur'd than it is. But to return to our present business; I cannot but commend both the kindness and prudence of a mother I knew, who was wont always to indulge her daughters, when any of them desired dogs, squirrels, birds, or any such things as young girls use to be delighted with: but then, when they had them, they must be sure to keep them well, and look diligently after them, that they wanted nothing, or were not ill used. For if they were negligent in their care of them, it was counted a great fault, which often forfeited their possession, or at least they fail'd not to be rebuked for it; whereby they were early taught diligence and good nature. And indeed, I think people should be accustomed, from their cradles, to be tender to all sensible creatures, and to spoil or *waste* nothing at all. This delight they take in *doing of mischief,* whereby I mean spoiling of any thing to no purpose, but more especially the pleasure they take to put any thing in pain, that is capable of it; I cannot persuade my self to be any other than a foreign and introduced disposition, an habit borrowed from custom and conversation. People teach children to strike, and laugh when they hurt or see harm come to others: and they have the examples of most about them, to confirm them in it. All the entertainment and talk of history is nothing almost but fighting and killing: and the honour and renown that is bestowed on conquerors (who for the most part are but the great butchers of mankind) farther mislead growing youth, who by this means come to think slaughter the laudable business of mankind, and the most heroic of virtues. By these steps unnatural cruelty is planted in us; and what humanity abhors, custom reconciles and recommends to us, by laying it in the way to honour. Thus, by fashion and opinion, that comes to be a pleasure, which in itself neither is, nor can be any. This ought carefully to be watched, and early remedied; so as to settle and cherish the contrary and more natural temper of benignity and *compassion* in the room of it; but still by the same gentle methods which are to be applied to the other two faults before mention'd. It may not perhaps be unreasonable here to add this farther caution, *viz.,* That the mischiefs or harms that come by play, inadvertency, or ignorance, and were not known to be harms, or design'd for mischief's sake, though they may perhaps be sometimes of considerable damage, yet are not at all, or but very gently, to be taken notice of. For this, I think, I cannot too often inculcate, that whatever miscarriage a child is guilty of, and whatever be the consequence of it, the thing to be regarded in taking notice of it, is only what root it springs from, and what habit it is like to establish: and to that the correction ought to be directed, and the child not to suffer any punishment for any harm which may have come by his play or inadvertency. The faults to be amended lie in the mind; and if they are such as either age will cure, or no ill habits will follow from, the present action, whatever displeasing circumstances it may have, is to be passed by without any animadversion.

117. Another way to instill sentiments of humanity, and to keep them lively in young folks, will be, to accustom them to civility in their language and deportment towards their inferiors and the meaner sort of people, particularly servants. It is not unusual to observe the children in gentlemen's families treat the servants of the house with domineering words, names of contempt, and an imperious carriage; as if they were of another race and species beneath them. Whether ill example, the advantage of fortune, or their natural vanity, inspire this haughtiness, it should be prevented, or weeded out; and a gentle, courteous, affable carriage towards the lower ranks of men, placed in the room of it. No part of their superiority will be hereby lost; but the distinction increased, and their authority strengthen'd; when love in inferiors is join'd to outward respect, and an esteem of the person has a share in their submission: and domestics will pay a more ready and chearful service, when they find themselves not spurn'd because fortune has laid them below the level of others at their master's feet. Children should not be suffer'd to lose the consideration of human nature in the shufflings of outward conditions. The more they have, the better humor'd they should be taught to be, and the more compassionate and gentle to those of their brethren who are placed lower, and have scantier portions. If they are suffer'd from their cradles to treat men ill and rudely, because, by their father's title, they think they have a little power over them, at best it is ill-bred; and if care be not taken, will by degrees nurse up their natural pride into an habitual contempt of those beneath them. And where will that probably end but in oppression and cruelty?

118. Curiosity in children (which I had occasion just to mention 108) is but an appetite after knowledge; and therefore ought to be encouraged in them, not only as a good sign, but as the great instrument nature has provided to remove that ignorance they were born with; and which, without this busy *inquisitiveness,* will make them dull and useless creatures. The ways to encourage it, and keep it active and busy, are, I suppose, these following:

1. Not to check or discountenance any *enquiries* he shall make, nor suffer them to be laugh'd at; but to *answer* all his *questions,* and *explain* the matter he desires to know, so as to make them as much

intelligible to him as suits the capacity of his age and knowledge. But confound not his understanding with explications or notions that are above it; or with the variety or number of things that are not to his present purpose. Mark what 'tis his mind aims at in the *question*, and not what words he expresses it in: and when you have informed and satisfied him in that, you shall see how his thoughts will enlarge themselves, and how by fit answers he may be led on farther than perhaps you could imagine. For knowledge is grateful to the understanding, as light to the eyes: children are pleased and delighted with it exceedingly, especially if they see that their *enquiries* are regarded, and that their desire of knowing is encouraged and commended. And I doubt not but one great reason why many children abandon themselves wholly to silly sports, and trifle away all their time insipidly, is, because they have found their *curiosity* baulk'd, and their *enquiries* neglected. But had they been treated with more kindness and respect, and their *questions* answered, as they should, to their satisfaction; I doubt not but they would have taken more pleasure in learning, and improving their knowledge, wherein there would be still newness and variety, which is what they are delighted with, than in returning over and over to the same play and play-things.

119. 2. To this serious answering their *questions,* and informing their understandings, in what they desire, as if it were a matter that needed it, should be added some peculiar ways of *commendation.* Let others whom they esteem, be told before their faces of the knowledge they have in such and such things; and since we are all, even from our cradles, vain and proud creatures, let their vanity be flatter'd with things that will do them good; and let their pride set them on work on something which may turn to their advantage. Upon this ground you shall find, that there cannot be a greater spur to the attaining what you would have the eldest learn, and know himself, than to set him upon *teaching* it *his younger brothers* and *sisters.*

120. 3. As children's *enquiries* are not to be slighted; so also great care is to be taken, that they *never* receive *deceitful* and *eluding answers.* They easily perceive when they are slighted or deceived; and quickly learn the trick of neglect, dissimulation and falsehood, which they observe others to make use of. We are not to intrench upon truth in any conversation, but least of all with children; since if we play false with them, we not only deceive their expectation, and hinder their knowledge, but corrupt their innocence, and teach them the worst of vices. They are travellers newly arrived in a strange country, of which they know nothing; we should therefore make conscience not to mislead them. And though their *questions* seem sometimes not very material, yet they should be seriously answer'd; for however they may appear to us (to whom they are long since known) *enquiries* not worth the making; they are of moment to those who are wholly ignorant. Children are strangers to all we are acquainted with; and all the things they meet with, are at first unknown to them, as they once were to us: and happy

are they who meet with civil people, that will comply with their ignorance, and help them to get out of it.

If you or I now should be set down in *Japan,* with all our prudence and knowledge about us, a conceit whereof makes us, perhaps, so apt to slight the thoughts and *enquiries* of children; should we, I say, be set down in *Japan,* we should, no doubt (if we would inform our selves of what is there to be known) ask a thousand questions, which, to a supercilious or inconsiderate *Japaner,* would seem very idle and impertinent; though to us they would be very material and of importance to be resolved; and we should be glad to find a man so complaisant and courteous, as to satisfy our demands, and instruct our ignorance.

When any new thing comes in their way, children usually ask the common *question* of a stranger: *What is it?* Whereby they ordinarily mean nothing but the name; and therefore to tell them how it is call'd, is usually the proper answer to that demand. And the next question usually is, *What is it for?* And to this it should be answered truly and directly. The use of the thing should be told, and the way explained, how it serves to such a purpose, as far as their capacities can comprehend it. And so of any other circumstances they shall ask about it; not turning them going, till you have given them all the satisfaction they are capable of; and so leading them by your answers into farther questions. And perhaps to a grown man, such conversation will not be altogether so idle and insignificant as we are apt to imagine. The native and untaught suggestions of inquisitive children do often offer things, that may set a considering man's thoughts on work. And I think there is frequently more to be learn'd from the unexpected questions of a child, than the discourses of men, who talk in a road, according to the notions they have borrowed, and the prejudices of their education.

Sections 121–130

121. 4. Perhaps it may not sometimes be amiss to excite their curiosity by bringing strange and new things in their way, on purpose to engage their enquiry, and give them occasion to inform themselves about them and if by chance their curiosity leads them to ask what they should not know, it is a great deal better to tell them plainly, that it is a thing that belongs not to them to know, than to pop them off with a falsehood of a frivolous answer.

122. *Pertness,* that appears sometimes so early, proceeds from a principle that seldom accompanies a strong constitution of body, or ripens into a strong judgment of mind. If it were desirable to have a child a more brisk talker, I believe there might be ways found to make him so: But I suppose a wise father had rather that his son should be able and useful, when a man, than pretty company, and a diversion to others, whilst a child: though if that too were to be consider'd, I think I may say, there is not so much pleasure to have a child prattle agreeably, as to reason well. Encourage therefore his *inquisitiveness* all you can, by satisfying his demands, and informing his judgment, as far as it is capable. When his reasons are any way tolerable, let him find the credit and commendation of it: and when they are quite out of the way, let him, without being laugh'd at for his mistake be gently put into the right; and if he shew a forwardness to be reasoning about things that come in his way, take care, as much as you can, that no body check this inclination in him, or mislead it by captious or fallacious ways of talking with him. For when all is done, this, as the highest and most important faculty of our minds, deserves the greatest care and attention in cultivating it: the right improvement, and exercise of our reason being the highest perfection that a man can attain to in this life.

123. Contrary to this busy inquisitive temper, there is sometimes observable in children, a *listless carelessness,* a want of regard to any thing, and a sort of *trifling* even at their business. This *sauntring* humour I look on as one of the worst qualities can appear in a child, as well as one of the hardest to be cured, where it is natural. But it being liable to be mistaken in some cases, care must be taken to make a right judgment concerning than trifling at their books or business, which may sometimes be complained of in a child. Upon the first suspicion a father has, that his son is of a *sauntring* temper, he must carefully observe him, whether he be *listless* and *indifferent* in all in his actions, or whether in some things alone he be slow and sluggish, but in others vigorous and eager. For tho' we find that he does loiter at his book, and

let a good deal of the time he spends in his chamber or study, run idly away; he must not presently conclude, that this is from a *sauntring* humour in his temper. It may be childishness, and a preferring something to his study, which his thoughts run on; and he dislikes his book, as is natural, because it is forced upon him as a task. To know this perfectly, you must watch him at play, when he is out of his place and time of study, following his own inclination; and see there whether he be stirring and active; whether he designs any thing, and with labour and eagerness pursues it, till he has accomplished what he aimed at, or whether he *lazily* and *listlessly dreams away his time.* If this sloth be only when he is about his book, I think it may be easily cured. If it be in his temper, it will require a little more pains and attention to remedy it.

124. If you are satisfied by his earnestness at play, or any thing else he sets his mind on, in the intervals between his hours of business, that he is not of himself inclined to *laziness,* but that only want of relish of his book makes him negligent and *sluggish* in his application to it; the first step is to try by talking to him kindly of the folly and inconvenience of it, whereby he loses a good part of his time, which he might have for his diversion: but be sure to talk calmly and kindly, and not much at first, but only these plain reasons in short. If this prevails, you have gain'd the point in the most desirable way, which is that of reason and kindness. If this softer application prevails not, try to shame him out of it, by laughing at him for it, asking every day, when he comes to table, if there be no strangers there, how long he was that day about his business: And if he has not done it in the time he might be well supposed to have dispatched it, expose and turn him into ridicule for it; but mix no chiding, only put on a pretty cold brow towards him, and keep it till he reform; and let his mother, tutor, and all about him do so too. If this work not the effect you desire, then tell him he shall be no longer troubled with a tutor to take care of his education, you will not be at the charge to have him spend his time idly with him; but since he prefers this or that [whatever play he delights in] to his book, that only he shall do; and so in earnest set him to work on his beloved play, and keep him steadily, and in earnest, to it morning and afternoon, till he be fully surfeited, and would, at any rate, change it for some hours at his book again. But when you thus set him his task of play, you must be sure to look after him your self, or set somebody else to do it, that may constantly see him employed in it, and that he be not permitted to be idle at that too. I say, your self look after him; for it is worth a father's while, whatever business he has, to bestow two or three days upon his son, to cure so great a mischief as his *sauntring* at his business.

125. This is what I propose, if it be *idleness,* not from his general temper, but a peculiar or acquir'd aversion to learning, which you must be careful to examine and distinguish. But though you have your eyes upon him, to watch what he does with the time which he has at his own disposal, yet you must not let him perceive that you or any body else do so; for that may hinder him from following his own inclination, which he being full of, and not daring, for fear of you, to prosecute what his head

and heart are set upon, he may neglect all other things, which then he relishes not, and so may seem to be idle and listless, when in truth it is nothing but being intent on that, which the fear of your eye or knowledge keeps him from executing. To be clear in this point, the observation must be made when you are out of the way, and he not so much as under the restraint of a suspicion that any body has an eye upon him. In those seasons of perfect freedom, let some body you can trust mark how he spends his time, whether he unactively loiters it away, when without any check he is left to his own inclination. Thus, by his employing of such times of liberty, you will easily discern, whether it be *listlessness* in his temper, or aversion to his book, that makes him *saunter* away his time of study.

126. If some defect in his constitution has cast a damp on his mind, and he be naturally listless and dreaming, this unpromising disposition is none of the easiest to be dealt with, because, generally carrying with it an unconcernedness for the future, it wants the two great springs of action, *foresight* and *desire;* which how to plant and increase, where nature has given a cold and contrary temper, will be the question. As soon as you are satisfied that this is the case, you must carefully enquire whether there be nothing he delights in; Inform your self what it is he is most pleased with; and if you can find any particular tendency his mind hath, increase it all you can, and make use of that to set him on work, and to excite his industry. If he loves praise, or play, or fine clothes, &c. or, on the other side, dreads pain, disgrace, or your displeasure, &c., whatever it be that he loves most, except it be sloth (for that will never set him on work) let that be made use of to quicken him, and make him bestir himself. For in this *listless temper,* you are not to fear an excess of appetite (as in all other cases) by cherishing it. 'Tis that which you want, and therefore must labour to raise and increase; for where there is no desire, there will be no industry.

127. If you have not hold enough upon him this way, to stir up vigour and activity in him, you must employ him in some constant bodily labour, whereby he may get an habit of doing something. The keeping him hard to some study were the better way to get him an habit of exercising and applying his mind. But because this is an invisible attention, and no body can tell when he is or is not idle at it, you must find bodily employments for him, which he must be constantly busied in, and kept to; and if they have some little hardship and shame in them, it may not be the worse, that they may the sooner weary him, and make him desire to return to his book. But be sure, when you exchange his book for his other labour, set him such a task, to be done in such a time as may allow him no opportunity to be idle. Only after you have by this way brought him to be attentive and industrious at his book, you may, upon his dispatching his study within the time set him, give him as a reward some respite from his other labour; which you may diminish as you find him grow more and more steady in his application, and at last wholly take off when his *sauntring* at his book is cured.

128. We formerly observed, that variety and freedom was that that delighted children, and recommended their plays to them; and that therefore their book or any thing we would have them learn, should not be enjoined them as *business*. This their parents, tutors, and teachers are apt to forget; and their impatience to have them busied in what is fit for them to do, suffers them not to deceive them into it: but by the repeated injunctions they meet with, children quickly distinguish between what is required of them, and what not. When this mistake has once made his book uneasy to him, the cure is to be applied at the other end. And since it will be then too late to endeavour to make it a play to him, you must take the contrary course: observe what play he is most delighted with; enjoin that, and make him play so many hours every day, not as a punishment for playing, but as if it were the business required of him. This, if I mistake not, will in a few days make him so weary of his most beloved sport, that he will prefer his book, or any thing to it, especially if it may redeem him from any part of the *task of play* is set him, and he may be suffered to employ some part of the time destined to his task of play in his book, or such other exercise as is really useful to him. This I at least think a better cure than that forbidding, (which usually increases the desire) or any other punishment should be made use of to remedy it: for when you have once glutted his appetite (which may safely be done in all things but eating and drinking) and made him surfeit of what you would have him avoid, you have put into him a principle of aversion, and you need not so much fear afterwards his longing for the same thing again.

129. This I think is sufficiently evident, that children generally hate to be idle. All the care then is, that their busy humour should be constantly employ'd in something of use to them; which, if you will attain, you must make what you would have them do a recreation to them, and not a *business*. The way to do this, so that they may not perceive you have any hand in it, is this proposed here; *viz.* To make them weary of that which you would not have them do, by enjoining and making them under some pretence or other do it, till they are surfeited. For example: Does your son play at top and scourge too much? Enjoin him to play so many hours every day, and look that he do it; and you shall see he will quickly be sick of it, and willing to leave it. By this means making the recreations you dislike a *business* to him, he will of himself with delight betake himself to those things you would have him do, especially if they be proposed as rewards for having performed his *task* in that play which is commanded him. For if he be ordered every day to whip his top so long as to make him sufficiently weary, do you not think he will apply himself with eagerness to his book, and wish for it, if you promise it him as a reward of having whipped his top lustily, quite out all the time that is set him? Children, in the things they do, if they comport with their age, find little difference so they may be doing: the esteem they have for one thing above another they borrow from others; so that what those about them make to be a reward to them, will really be so. By this art it is in their governor's choice, whether *scotchhoppers* shall reward their *dancing*, or *dancing* their *scotchhoppers*; whether peg-top, or

reading; playing at trap, or studying the globes, shall be more acceptable and pleasing to them; all that they desire being to be busy, and busy, as they imagine, in things of their own choice, and which they receive as favours from their parents or others for whom they have respect and with whom they would be in credit. A set of children thus ordered and kept from the ill example of others, would all of them, I suppose, with as much earnestness and delight, learn to read, write, and what else one would have them, as others do their ordinary plays: and the eldest being thus entered, and this made the fashion of the place, it would be as impossible to hinder them from learning the one, as it is ordinarily to keep them from the other.

130. Play-things, I think, children should have, and of divers sorts; but still to be in the custody of their tutors or some body else, whereof the child should have in his power but one at once, and should not be suffered to have another but when he restored that. This teaches them betimes to be careful of not losing or spoiling the things they have; whereas plenty and variety in their own keeping, makes them wanton and careless, and teaches them from the beginning to be squanderers and wasters. These, I confess, are little things, and such as will seem beneath the care of a governor; but nothing that may form children's minds is to be overlooked and neglected, and whatsoever introduces habits, and settles customs in them, deserves the care and attention of their governors, and is not a small thing in its consequences.

One thing more about children's play-things may be worth their parents' care. Though it be agreed they should have of several sorts, yet, I think, they should have none bought for them. This will hinder that great variety they are often overcharged with, which serves only to teach the mind to wander after change and superfluity, to be unquiet, and perpetually stretching itself after something more still, though it knows not what, and never to be satisfied with what it hath. The court that is made to people of condition in such kind of presents to their children, does the little ones great harm. By it they are taught pride, vanity and covetousness, almost before they can speak: and I have known a young child so distracted with the number and variety of his play-games, that he tired his maid every day to look them over; and was so accustomed to abundance, that he never thought he had enough, but was always asking, What more? What more? What new thing shall I have? A good introduction to moderate desires, and the ready way to make a contented happy man!

"How then shall they have the play-games you allow them, if none must be bought for them?" I answer, they should make them themselves, or at least endeavour it, and set themselves about it; till then they should have none, and till then they will want none of any great artifice. A smooth pebble, a piece of paper, the mother's bunch of keys, or any thing they cannot hurt themselves with, serves as much to divert little children as those more chargeable and curious toys from the shops, which are presently put out of order and broken. Children are never dull, or out of humour, for want of such playthings, unless they have been used to them; when they are little, whatever occurs serves the turn; and as they grow bigger, if they are not stored by the expensive folly of others, they will make them themselves. Indeed, when they once begin to set themselves to work about any of their inventions, they should be taught and assisted; but should have nothing whilst they lazily sit still, expecting to be furnish'd from other hands, without employing their own. And if you help them where they are at a stand, it will more endear you to them than any chargeable toys you shall buy for them. Play-things which are above their skill to make, as tops, gigs, battledores, and the like, which are to be used with labour, should indeed be procured them. These 'tis convenient they should have, not for variety but exercise; but these too should be given them as bare as might be. If they had a top, the scourge-stick and leather-strap should be left to their own making and fitting. If they sit gaping to have such things drop into their mouths, they should go without them. This will accustom them to seek for what they want, in themselves and in their own endeavours; whereby they will be taught moderation in their desires, application, industry, thought, contrivance, and good husbandry; qualities that will be useful to them when they are men, and therefore cannot be learned too soon, nor fixed too deep. All the plays and diversions of children should be directed towards good and useful habits, or else they will introduce ill ones. Whatever they do, leaves some impression on that tender age, and from thence they receive a tendency to good or evil: and whatever hath such an influence, ought not to be neglected.

Sections 131–140

131. *Lying* is so ready and cheap a cover for any miscarriage, and so much in fashion among all sorts of people, that a child can hardly avoid observing the use is made of it on all occasions, and so can scarce be kept without great care from getting into it. But it is so ill a quality, and the mother of so many ill ones that spawn from it, and take shelter under it, that a child should be brought up in the greatest abhorrence of it imaginable. It should be always (when occasionally it comes to be mention'd) spoke of before him with the utmost detestation, as a quality so wholly inconsistent with the name and character of a gentleman, that no body of any credit can bear the imputation of a lie; a mark that is judg'd the utmost disgrace, which debases a man to the lowest degree of a shameful meanness, and ranks him with the most contemptible part of mankind and the abhorred rascality; and is not to be endured in any one who would converse with people of condition, or have any esteem or reputation in the world. The first time he is found in a *lie*, it should rather be wondered at as a monstrous thing in him, than reproved as an ordinary fault. If that keeps him not from relapsing, the next time he must be sharply rebuked, and fall into the state of great displeasure of his father and mother and all about him who take notice of it. And if this way work not the cure, you must come to blows; for after he has been thus warned, a premeditated *lie* must always be looked upon as obstinacy, and never be permitted to escape unpunished.

132. Children, afraid to have their faults seen in their naked colours, will, like the rest of the sons of *Adam,* be apt to make *excuses.* This is a fault usually bordering upon, and leading to untruth, and is not to be indulged in them; but yet it ought to be cured rather with shame than roughness. If therefore, when a child is questioned for any thing, his first answer be an *excuse,* warn him soberly to tell the truth; and then if he persists to shuffle it off with a *falsehood,* he must be chastised; but if he directly confess, you must commend his ingenuity, and pardon the fault, be it what it will; and pardon it so, that you never so much as reproach him with it, or mention it to him again: for if you would have him in love with ingenuity, and by a constant practice make it habitual to him, you must take care that it never procure him the least inconvenience; but on the contrary, his own confession bringing always with it perfect impunity, should be besides encouraged by some marks of approbation. If his *excuse* be such at any time that you cannot prove it to have any falsehood in it, let it pass for true, and be sure not to shew any suspicion of it. Let him keep up his reputation with you as high as is possible; for when once he finds he has lost that, you have

lost a great, and your best hold upon him. Therefore let him not think he has the character of a liar with you, as long as you can avoid it without flattering him in it. Thus some slips in truth may be overlooked. But after he has once been corrected for a *lie,* you must be sure never after to pardon it in him, whenever you find and take notice to him that he is guilty of it: for it being a fault which he has been forbid, and may, unless he be wilful, avoid, the repeating of it is perfect perverseness, and must have the chastisement due to that offence.

133. This is what I have thought concerning the general method of educating a young gentleman; which, though I am apt to suppose may have some influence on the whole course of his education, yet I am far from imagining it contains all those particulars which his growing years or peculiar temper may require. But this being premised in general, we shall in the next place, descend to a more particular consideration of the several parts of his education.

134. That which every gentleman (that takes any care of his education) desires for his son, besides the estate he leaves him, is contain'd (I suppose) in these four things, *virtue, wisdom, breeding* and *learning.* I will not trouble my self whether these names do not some of them sometimes stand for the same thing, or really include one another. It serves my turn here to follow the popular use of these words, which, I presume, is clear enough to make me be understood, and I hope there will be no difficulty to comprehend my meaning.

135. I place *virtue* as the first and most necessary of those endowments that belong to a man or a gentleman; as absolutely requisite to make him valued and beloved by others, acceptable or tolerable to himself. Without that, I think, he will be happy neither in this nor the other world.

136. As the foundation of this, there ought very early to be imprinted on his mind a true notion of *God,* as of the independent Supreme Being, Author and Maker of all things, from Whom we receive all our good, Who loves us, and gives us all things. And consequent to this, instil into him a love and reverence of this Supreme Being. This is enough to begin with, without going to explain this matter any farther; for fear lest by talking too early to him of spirits, and being unseasonably forward to make him understand the incomprehensible nature of that Infinite Being, his head be either fill'd with false, or perplex'd with unintelligible notions of Him. Let him only be told upon occasion, that *God* made and governs all things, hears and sees every thing, and does all manner of good to those that love and obey Him; you will find, that being told of such a *God,* other thoughts will be apt to rise up fast enough in his mind about Him; which, as you observe them to have any mistakes, you must set right. And I think it would be better if men generally rested in such an idea of *God,* without being too curious in their notions about a Being which all must acknowledge incomprehensible; whereby many, who have not strength and clearness of thought to distinguish between what

they can, and what they cannot know, run themselves in superstitions or atheism, making *God* like themselves, or (because they cannot comprehend any thing else) none at all. And I am apt to think, the keeping children constantly morning and evening to acts of devotion to God, as to their Maker, Preserver and Benefactor, in some plain and short form of prayer, suitable to their age and capacity, will be of much more use to them in religion, knowledge, and virtue, than to distract their thoughts with curious enquiries into His inscrutable essence and being.

137. Having by gentle degrees, as you find him capable of it, settled such an idea of God in his mind, and taught him to *pray* to Him, and *praise* Him as the Author of his being, and of all the good he does or can enjoy; forbear any discourse of other *spirits*, till the mention of them coming in his way, upon occasion hereafter to be set down, and his reading the scripture-history, put him upon that enquiry.

138. But even then, and always whilst he is young, be sure to preserve his tender mind from all impressions and notions of *spirits* and *goblins,* or any fearful apprehensions in the dark. This he will be in danger of from the indiscretion of servants, whose usual method is to awe children, and keep them in subjection, by telling them of *raw-head* and *bloody-bones,* and such other names as carry with them the ideas of something terrible and hurtful, which they have reason to be afraid of when alone, especially in the dark. This must be carefully prevented: for though by this foolish way, they may keep them from little faults, yet the remedy is much worse than the disease; and there are stamped upon their imaginations ideas that follow them with terror and affrightment. Such *bug-bear* thoughts once got into the tender minds of children, and being set on with a strong impression from the dread that accompanies such apprehensions, sink deep, and fasten themselves so as not easily, if ever, to be got out again; and whilst they are there, frequently haunt them with strange visions, making children dastards when alone, and afraid of their shadows and darkness all their lives after. I have had those complain to me, when men, who had been thus used when young; that though their reason corrected the wrong ideas they had taken in, and they were satisfied that there was no cause to fear invisible beings more in the dark than in the light, yet that these notions were apt still upon any occasion to start up first in their prepossessed fancies, and not to be removed without some pains. And to let you see how lasting and frightful images are, that take place in the mind early, I shall here tell you a pretty remarkable but true story. There was in a town in the *west* a man of a disturbed brain, whom the boys used to teaze when he came in their way: this fellow one day seeing in the street one of those lads, that used to vex him, stepped into a *cutler's* shop he was near, and there seizing on a naked sword, made after the boy; who seeing him coming so armed, betook himself to his feet, and ran for his life, and by good luck had strength and heels enough to reach his father's house before the mad-man could get up to him. The door was only latch'd; and when he had the latch in his hand,

he turn'd about his head, to see how near his pursuer was, who was at the entrance of the porch, with his sword up ready to strike; and he had just time to get in, and clap to the door to avoid the blow, which, though his body escaped, his mind did not. This frightening idea made so deep an impression there, that it lasted many years, if not all his life after. For, telling this story when he was a man, he said, that after that time till then, he never went in at that door (that he could remember) at any time without looking back, whatever business he had in his head, or how little soever before he came thither he thought of this mad-man.

If children were let alone, they would be no more afraid in the dark, than in broad sun-shine; they would in their turns as much welcome the one for sleep as the other to play in. There should be no distinction made to them by any discourse of more danger or *terrible things* in the one than the other: but if the folly of any one about them should do them this harm, and make them think there is any difference between being in the dark and winking, you must get it out of their minds as soon as you can; and let them know, that God, who made all things good for them, made the night that they might sleep the better and the quieter; and that they being under his protection, there is nothing in the dark to hurt them. What is to be known more of God and good spirits, is to be deferr'd till the time we shall hereafter mention; and of evil spirits, 'twill be well if you can keep him from wrong fancies about them till he is ripe for that sort of knowledge.

139. Having laid the foundations of virtue in a true notion of a God, such as the creed wisely teaches, as far as his age is capable, and by accustoming him to pray to Him; the next thing to be taken care of is to keep him exactly to speaking of *truth,* and by all the ways imaginable inclining him to be *good-natur'd.* Let him know that twenty faults are sooner to be forgiven than the *straining of truth* to cover any one *by an excuse.* And to teach him betimes to love and be *good-natur'd* to others, is to lay early the true foundation of an honest man; all injustice generally springing from too great love of ourselves and too little of others.

This is all I shall say of this matter in general, and is enough for laying the first foundations of virtue in a child: as he grows up, the tendency of his natural inclination must be observed; which, as it inclines him more than is convenient on one or t'other side from the right path of virtue, ought to have proper remedies applied. For few of *Adam's* children are so happy, as not to be born with some byass in their natural temper, which it is the business of education either to take off, or counterbalance. But to enter into particulars of this, would be beyond the design of this short treatise of education. I intend not a discourse of all the virtues and vices, how each virtue is to be attained, and every particular vice by its peculiar remedies cured: though I have mentioned some of the most ordinary faults, and the ways to be used in correcting them.

110

140. *Wisdom* I take in the popular acceptation, for a man's managing his business ably and with foresight in this world. This is the product of a good natural temper, application of mind, and experience together, and so above the reach of children. The greatest thing that in them can be done towards it, is to hinder them, as much as may be, from being *cunning;* which, being the ape of *wisdom,* is the most distant from it that can be: and as an ape for the likeness it has to a man, wanting what really should make him so, is by so much the uglier; *cunning* is only the want of understanding, which because it cannot compass its ends by direct ways, would do it by a trick and circumvention; and the mischief of it is, a *cunning* trick helps but once, but hinders ever after. No cover was ever made so big or so fine as to hide it self: no body was ever so *cunning* as to conceal their being so: and when they are once discovered, every body is shy, every body distrustful of *crafty* men; and all the world forwardly join to oppose and defeat them; whilst the open, fair, *wise* man has every body to make way for him, and goes directly to his business. To accustom a child to have true notions of things, and not to be satisfied till he has them; to raise his mind to great and worthy thoughts, and to keep him at a distance from falsehood and cunning, which has always a broad mixture of falsehood in it; is the fittest preparation of a child for *wisdom.* The rest, which is to be learn'd from time, experience, and observation, and an acquaintance with men, their tempers and designs, is not to be expected in the ignorance and inadvertency of childhood, or the inconsiderate heat and unweariness of youth: all that can be done towards it, during this unripe age, is, as I have said, to accustom them to truth and sincerity; to a submission to reason; and as much as may be, to reflection on their own actions.

Sections 141–150

141. The next good quality belonging to a gentleman, is *good breeding*. There are two sorts of *ill-breeding:* the one a *sheepish bashfulness,* and the other a *mis-becoming negligence and disrespect* in our carriage; both which are avoided by duly observing this one rule, *not to think meanly of ourselves, and not to think meanly of others.*

142. The first part of this rule must not be understood in opposition to humility, but to assurance. We ought not to think so well of our selves, as to stand upon our own value; and assume to our selves a preference before others, because of any advantage we may imagine we have over them; but modestly to take what is offered, when it is our due. But yet we ought to think so well of our selves, as to perform those actions which are incumbent on, and expected of us, without discomposure or disorder, in whose presence soever we are; keeping that respect and distance which is due to every one's rank and quality. There is often in people, especially children, a clownish shamefacedness before strangers or those above them: they are confounded in their thoughts, words, and looks; and so lose themselves in that confusion as not to be able to do any thing, or at least not to do it with that freedom and gracefulness which pleases, and makes them be acceptable. The only cure for this, as for any other miscarriage, is by use to introduce the contrary habit. But since we cannot accustom ourselves to converse with strangers and persons of quality without being in their company, nothing can cure this part of *ill-breeding* but change and variety of company, and that of persons above us.

143. As the before-mentioned consists in too great a concern how to behave ourselves towards others; so the other part of *ill-breeding* lies in the appearance of too *little care* of pleasing or *shewing respect* to those we have to do with. To avoid this these two things are requisite: first, a disposition of the mind not to offend others; and secondly, the most acceptable and agreeable way of expressing that disposition. From the one men are called *civil;* from the other *well-fashion'd.* The latter of these is that decency and gracefulness of looks, voice, words, motions, gestures, and of all the whole outward demeanour, which takes in company, and makes those with whom we may converse, easy and well pleased. This is, as it were, the language whereby that internal civility of the mind is expressed; which, as other languages are, being very much governed by the fashion and custom of every country, must, in the rules and practice of it, be learn'd chiefly from observation, and the carriage of those who are allow'd to be exactly *well-bred.* The other part, which

lies deeper than the outside, is that general good-will and regard for all people, which makes any one have a care not to shew in his carriage any contempt, disrespect, or neglect of them; but to express, according to the fashion and way of that country, a respect and value for them according to their rank and condition. It is a disposition of the mind that shews it self in the carriage, whereby a man avoids making any one uneasy in conversation.

I shall take notice of four qualities, that are most directly opposite to this first and most taking of all the social virtues. And from some one of these four it is, that incivility commonly has its rise. I shall set them down, that children may be preserv'd or recover'd from their ill influence.

1. The first is, a natural *roughness,* which makes a man uncomplaisant to others, so that he has no deference for their inclinations, tempers, or conditions. 'Tis the sure badge of a clown, not to mind what pleases or displeases those he is with; and yet one may often find a man in fashionable clothes give an unbounded swing to his own humour, and suffer it to justle or over-run any one that stands in its way, with a perfect indifferency how they take it. This is a brutality that every one sees and abhors, and nobody can be easy with: and therefore this finds no place in any one who would be thought to have the least tincture of *good-breeding.* For the very end and business of *good-breeding* is to supple the natural stiffness, and so soften men's tempers, that they may bend to a compliance, and accommodate themselves to those they have to do with.

2. *Contempt,* or want of due respect, discovered either in looks, words, or gesture: this, from whomsoever it comes, brings always uneasiness with it. For nobody can contentedly bear being slighted.

3. *Censoriousness,* and finding fault with others, has a direct opposition to *civility.* Men, whatever they are or are not guilty of, would not have their faults display'd and set in open view and broad day-light, before their own or other people's eyes. Blemishes affixed to any one always carry shame with them: and the discovery, or even bare imputation of any defect is not borne without some uneasiness. *Raillery* is the most refined way of exposing the faults of others: but, because it is usually done with wit and good language, and gives entertainment to the company, people are led into a mistake, that where it keeps within fair bounds there is no incivility in it. And so the pleasantry of this sort of conversation often introduces it amongst people of the better rank; and such talkers are favourably heard and generally applauded by the laughter of the bystanders on their side. But they ought to consider, that the entertainment of the rest of the company is at the cost of that one who is set out in their burlesque colours, who therefore is not without uneasiness, unless the subject for which he is rallied be really in itself matter of commendation. For then the pleasant images and representations which make the *raillery* carrying praise as well as sport

with them, the rallied person also finds his account, and takes part in the diversion. But because the right management of so nice and ticklish a business, wherein a little slip may spoil all, is not every body's talent, I think those who would secure themselves from provoking others, especially all young people, should carefully abstain from *raillery,* which by a small mistake or any wrong turn, may leave upon the mind of those who are made uneasy by it, the lasting memory of having been piquantly, tho' wittily, taunted for some thing censurable in them.

Besides raillery, *contradiction* is a sort of censoriousness wherein ill-breeding often shews it self. Complaisance does not require that we should always admit all the reasonings or relations that the company is entertain'd with, no, nor silently to let pass all that is vented in our hearing. The opposing the opinions, and rectifying the mistakes of others, is what truth and charity sometimes require of us, and civility does not oppose, if it be done with due caution and care of circumstances. But there are some people, that one may observe, possessed as it were with the spirit of contradiction, that steadily, and without regard to right or wrong, oppose some one, or, perhaps, every one of the company, whatever they say. This is so visible and outrageous a way of *censuring,* that nobody can avoid thinking himself injur'd by it. All opposition to what another man has said, is so apt to be suspected of *censoriousness,* and is so seldom received without some sort of humiliation, that it ought to be made in the gentlest manner, and softest words can be found, and such as with the whole deportment may express no forwardness to contradict. All marks of respect and good will ought to accompany it, that whilst we gain the argument, we may not lose the esteem of those that hear us.

4. *Captiousness* is another fault opposite to civility; not only because it often produces misbecoming and provoking expressions and carriage; but because it is a tacit accusation and reproach of some incivility taken notice of in those whom we are angry with. Such a suspicion or intimation cannot be borne by any one without uneasiness. Besides, one angry body discomposes the whole company, and the harmony ceases upon any such jarring.

The happiness that all men so steadily pursue consisting in pleasure, it is easy to see why the *civil* are more acceptable than the useful. The ability, sincerity, and good intention of a man of weight and worth, or a real friend, seldom atones for the uneasiness that is produced by his grave and solid representations. Power and riches, nay virtue itself, are valued only as conducing to our happiness. And therefore he recommends himself ill to another as aiming at his happiness, who, in the services he does him, makes him uneasy in the manner of doing them. He that knows how to make those he converses with easy, without debasing himself to low and servile flattery, has found the true art of living in the world, and being both welcome and valued every where. *Civility* therefore is what in the first place should with great care be made habitual to children and young people.

144. There is another fault in good manners, and that is *excess of ceremony,* and an obstinate persisting to force upon another what is not his due, and what he cannot take without folly or shame. This seems rather a design to expose than oblige: or at least looks like a contest for mastery, and at best is but troublesome, and so can be no part of *good-breeding,* which has no other use or end but to make people easy and satisfied in their conversation with us. This is a fault few young people are apt to fall into; but yet if they are ever guilty of it, or are suspected to incline that way, they should be told of it, and warned of this *mistaken civility.* The thing they should endeavour and aim at in conversation, should be to shew respect, esteem, and good-will, by paying to every one that common ceremony and regard which is in civility due to them. To do this without a suspicion of flattery, dissimulation, or meanness, is a great skill, which good sense, reason, and good company can only teach; but is of so much use in civil life that it is well worth the studying.

145. Though the managing ourselves well in this part of our behaviour has the name of *good-breeding,* as if peculiarly the effect of education; yet, as I have said, young children should not be much perplexed about it; I mean, about putting off their hats, and making legs modishly. Teach them humility, and to be good-natur'd, if you can, and this sort of manners will not be wanting; *civility* being in truth nothing but a care not to shew any slighting or contempt of any one in conversation. What are the most allow'd and esteem'd ways of expressing this, we have above observ'd. It is as peculiar and different, in several countries of the world, as their languages; and therefore, if it be rightly considered, rules and discourses made to children about it, are as useless and impertinent, as it would be now and then to give a rule or two of the *Spanish* tongue to one that converses only with *Englishmen.* Be as busy as you please with discourses of *civility* to your son, such as is his company, such will be his manners. A plough-man of your neighbourhood that has never been out of his parish, read what lectures you please to him, will be as soon in his language as his carriage a courtier; that is, in neither will be more polite than those he uses to converse with: and therefore, of this no other care can be taken till he be of an age to have a tutor put to him, who must not fail to be a well-bred man. And, in good earnest, if I were to speak my mind freely, so children do nothing out of obstinacy, pride, and ill-nature, 'tis no great matter how they put off their hats or make legs. If you can teach them to love and respect other people, they will, as their age requires it, find ways to express it acceptably to every one, according to the fashions they have been used to: and as to their motions and carriage of their bodies, a dancing-master, as has been said, when it is fit, will teach them what is most becoming. In the mean time, when they are young, people expect not that children should be over-mindful of these ceremonies; carelessness is allow'd to that age, and becomes them as well as compliments do grown people: or, at least, if some very nice people will think it a fault, I am sure it is a fault that should be over-

look'd, and left to time, a tutor and conversation to cure. And therefore I think it not worth your while to have your son (as I often see children are) molested or chid about it: but where there is *pride* or *ill-nature* appearing in his carriage, there he must be persuaded or shamed out of it.

Though children, when little, should not be much perplexed with rules and ceremonious parts of *breeding,* yet there is a sort of unmannerliness very apt to grow up with young people, if not early restrained, and that is, a forwardness to *interrupt* others that are speaking; and to stop them with some *contradiction.* Whether the custom of disputing, and the reputation of parts and learning usually given to it as if it were the only standard and evidence of knowledge, make young men so forward to watch occasions to correct others in their discourse, and not to slip any opportunity of shewing their talents: so it is, that I have found scholars most blamed in this point. There cannot be a greater rudeness, than to *interrupt* another in the current of his discourse; for if there be not impertinent folly in answering a man before we know what he will say, yet it is a plain declaration, that we are weary to hear him talk any longer, and have a dis-esteem of what he says; which we judging not fit to entertain the company, desire them to give audience to us, who have something to produce worth their attention. This shews a very great disrespect, and cannot but be offensive: and yet this is what almost all interruption constantly carries with it. To which, if there be added, as is usual, a *correcting* of any mistake, or a *contradiction* of what has been said, it is a mark of yet greater pride and self-conceitedness, when we thus intrude our selves for teachers, and take upon us either to set another right in his story, or shew the mistakes of his judgment.

I do not say this, that I think there should be no difference of opinions in conversation, nor opposition in men's discourses: this would be to take away the greatest advantage of society, and the improvements are to be made by ingenious company; where the light is to be got from the opposite arguings of men of parts, shewing the different sides of things and their various aspects and probabilities, would be quite lost, if every one were obliged to assent to, and say after the first speaker. 'Tis not the owning one's dissent from another, that I speak against, but the manner of doing it. Young men should be taught not to be forward to *interpose* their opinions, unless asked, or when others have done, and are silent; and then only by way of enquiry, not instruction. The positive asserting, and the magisterial air should be avoided; and when a general pause of the whole company affords an opportunity, they may modestly put in their question as learners.

This becoming decency will not cloud their parts, nor weaken the strength of their reason; but bespeak the more favourable attention, and give what they say the greater advantage. An ill argument, or ordinary observation, thus introduc'd, with some civil preface of deference and respect to the opinions of others, will procure them more credit and esteem than the sharpest wit, or profoundest science, with a rough, insolent, or noisy management, which always shocks the hearers, leaves an ill opinion of the man, though he get the better of it in the argument.

This therefore should be carefully watched in young people, stopp'd in the beginning, and the contrary habit introduced in all their conversation. And the rather, because forwardness to talk, frequent *interruptions* in arguing, and loud *wrangling,* are too often observable amongst grown people, even of rank, amongst us. The *Indians,* whom we call barbarous, observe much more decency and civility in their discourses and conversation, giving one another a fair silent hearing till they have quite done; and then answering them calmly, and without noise or passion. And if it be not so in this civiliz'd part of the world, we must impute it to a neglect in education, which has not yet reform'd this antient piece of barbarity amongst us. Was it not, think you, an entertaining spectacle, to see two ladies of quality accidentally seated on the opposite sides of a room, set round with company, fall into a dispute, and grow so eager in it, that in the heat of the controversy, edging by degrees their chairs forwards, they were in a little time got up close to one another in the middle of the room; where they for a good while managed the dispute as fiercely as two game-cocks in the pit, without minding or taking any notice of the circle, which could not all the while forbear smiling? This I was told by a person of quality, who was present at the combat, and did not omit to reflect upon the indecencies that warmth in *dispute* often runs people into; which, since custom makes too frequent, education should take the more care of. There is no body but condemns this in others, though they overlook it in themselves; and many who are sensible of it in themselves, and resolve against it, cannot yet get rid of an ill custom, which neglect in their education has suffer'd to settle into an habit.

146. What has been above said concerning *company,* would perhaps, if it were well reflected on, give us a larger prospect, and let us see how much farther its influence reaches. 'Tis not the modes of civility alone, that are imprinted by *conversation:* the tincture of company sinks deeper than the out-side; and possibly, if a true estimate were made of the morality and religions of the world, we should find that the far greater part of mankind received even those opinions, and ceremonies they would die for, rather from the fashions of their countries, and the constant practice of those about them, than from any conviction of their reasons. I mention this only to let you see of what moment I think *company* is to your son in all the parts of his life, and therefore how much that one part is to be weighed and provided for; it being of greater force to work upon him, than all you can do besides.

147. You will wonder, perhaps, that I put *learning* last, especially if I tell you I think it the least part. This may seem strange in the mouth of a bookish man; and this making usually the chief, if not only bustle and stir about children, this being almost that alone which is thought on,

when people talk of education, makes it the greater paradox. When I consider, what ado is made about a little *Latin* and *Greek,* how many years are spent in it, and what a noise and business it makes to no purpose, I can hardly forbear thinking that the parents of children still live in fear of the school-master's rod, which they look on as the only instrument of education; as a language or two to be its whole business. How else is it possible that a child should be chain'd to the oar seven, eight, or ten of the best years of his life, to get a language or two, which, I think, might be had at a great deal cheaper rate of pains and time, and be learn'd almost in playing?

Forgive me therefore if I say, I cannot with patience think, that a young gentleman should be put into the herd, and be driven with a whip and scourge, as if he were to run the gantlet through the several classes, *ad capiendum ingenii cultum.* What then? say you, would you not have him write and read? Shall he be more ignorant than the clerk of our parish, who takes *Hopkins* and *Sternhold* for the best poets in the world, whom yet he makes worse than they are by his ill reading? Not so, not so fast, I beseech you. Reading and writing and *learning* I allow to be necessary, but yet not the chief business. I imagine you would think him a very foolish fellow, that should not value a virtuous or a wise man infinitely before a great scholar. Not but that I think *learning* a great help to both in well-dispos'd minds; but yet it must be confess'd also, that in others not so dispos'd, it helps them only to be the more foolish, or worse men. I say this, that when you consider the breeding of your son, and are looking out for a school-master or a tutor, you would not have (as is usual) Latin and *logick* only in your thoughts. *Learning* must be had, but in the second place, as subservient only to greater qualities. Seek out somebody that may know how discreetly to frame his manners: place him in hands where you may, as much as possible, secure his innocence, cherish and nurse up the good, and gently correct and weed out any bad inclinations, and settle in him good habits. This is the main point, and this being provided for, *learning* may be had into the bargain, and that, as I think, at a very easy rate, by methods that may be thought on.

148. When he can talk, 'tis time he should begin to *learn to read.* But as to this, give me leave here to inculcate again, what is very apt to be forgotten, *viz.* That great care is to be taken, that it be never made as a business to him, nor he look on it as a task. We naturally, as I said, even from our cradles, love liberty, and have therefore an aversion to many things for no other reason but because they are enjoin'd us. I have always had a fancy that *learning* might be made a play and recreation to children: and that they might be brought to desire to be taught, if it were proposed to them as a thing of honour, credit, delight, and recreation, or as a reward for doing something else; and if they were never chid or corrected for the neglect of it. That which confirms me in this opinion is, that amongst the *Portuguese,* 'tis so much a fashion and emulation amongst their children, to *learn to read* and write, that they cannot hinder them from it: they will learn it one from

another, and are as intent on it, as if it were forbidden them. I remember that being at a friend's house, whose younger son, a child in coats, was not easily *brought* to his book (being taught *to read* at home by his mother) I advised to try another way, than requiring it of him as his duty; we therefore, in a discourse on purpose amongst our selves, in his hearing, but without taking any notice of him, declared, that it was the privilege and advantage of heirs and elder brothers, to be scholars; that this made them fine gentlemen, and beloved by every body: and that for younger brothers, 'twas a favour to admit them to breeding; to be taught to *read* and write, was more than came to their share; they might be ignorant bumpkins and clowns, if they pleased. This so wrought upon the child, that afterwards he desired to be taught; would come himself to his mother to *learn,* and would not let his maid be quiet till she heard him his lesson. I doubt not but some way like this might be taken with other children; and when their tempers are found, some thoughts be instill'd into them, that might set them upon desiring of *learning,* themselves, and make them seek it as another sort of play or recreation. But then, as I said before, it must never be imposed as a task, nor made a trouble to them. There may be dice and play-things, with the letters on them to teach children the *alphabet* by playing; and twenty other ways may be found, suitable to their particular tempers, to make this kind of *learning a sport* to them.

149. Thus children may be cozen'd into a knowledge of the letters; be *taught to read,* without perceiving it to be any thing but a sport, and play themselves into that which others are whipp'd for. Children should not have any thing like work, or serious, laid on them; neither their minds, nor bodies will bear it. It injures their healths; and their being forced and tied down to their books in an age at enmity with all such restraint, has, I doubt not, been the reason, why a great many have hated books and learning all their lives after. 'Tis like a surfeit, that leaves an aversion behind not to be removed.

150. I have therefore thought, that if *play-things* were fitted to this purpose, as they are usually to none, contrivances might be made to *teach children to read,* whilst they thought they were only playing. For example, what if an *ivory-ball* were made like that of the royal-oak lottery, with thirty two sides, or one rather of twenty four or twenty five sides; and upon several of those sides pasted on an A, upon several others B, on others C, and on others D? I would have you begin with but these four letters, or perhaps only two at first; and when he is perfect in them, then add another; and so on till each side having one letter, there be on it the whole alphabet. This I would have others play with before him, it being as good a sort of play to lay a stake who shall first throw an A or B, as who upon dice shall throw six or seven. This being a play amongst you, tempt him not to it, lest you make it business; for I would not have him understand 'tis any thing but a play of older people, and I doubt not but he will take to it of himself. And that he may have the more reason to think it is a play, that he is sometimes in favour admitted to, when the play is done the ball should be laid up safe out of

his reach, that so it may not, by his having it in his keeping at any time, grow stale to him.

Sections 151–160

151. To keep up his eagerness to it, let him think it a game belonging to those above him: and when, by this means, he knows the letters, by changing them into syllables, he may *learn to read*, without knowing how he did so, and never have any chiding or trouble about it, nor fall out with books because of the hard usage and vexation they have caus'd him. Children, if you observe them, take abundance of pains to learn several games, which, if they should be enjoined them, they would abhor as a task and business. I know a person of great quality (more yet to be honoured for his learning and virtue than for his rank and high place) who by pasting on the six vowels (for in our language Y is one) on the six sides of a die, and the remaining eighteen consonants on the sides of three other dice, has made this a play for his children, that he shall win who, at one cast, throws most words on these four dice; whereby his eldest son, yet in coats, has *play'd* himself *into spelling*, with great eagerness, and without once having been chid for it or forced to it.

152. I have seen little girls exercise whole hours together and take abundance of pains to be expert at *dibstones* as they call it. Whilst I have been looking on, I have thought it wanted only some good contrivance to make them employ all that industry about something that might be more useful to them; and methinks 'tis only the fault and negligence of elder people that it is not so. Children are much less apt to be idle than men; and men are to be blamed if some part of that busy humour be not turned to useful things; which might be made usually as delightful to them as those they are employed in, if men would be but half so forward to lead the way, as these little apes would be to follow. I imagine some wise *Portuguese* heretofore began this fashion amongst the children of his country, where I have been told, as I said, it is impossible to hinder the children from *learning to read and write:* and in some parts of *France* they teach one another to sing and dance from the cradle.

153. The *letters* pasted upon the sides of the dice, or polygon, were best to be of the size of those of the folio Bible, to begin with, and none of them capital letters; when once he can read what is printed in such letters, he will not long be ignorant of the great ones: and in the beginning he should not be perplexed with variety. With this die also, you might have a play just like the royal oak, which would be another variety, and play for cherries or apples, &c.

123

154. Besides these, twenty other plays might be invented depending on *letters,* which those who like this way, may easily contrive and get made to this use if they will. But the four dice above-mention'd I think so easy and useful, that it will be hard to find any better, and there will be scarce need of any other.

155. Thus much for *learning to read,* which let him never be driven to, nor chid for; cheat him into it if you can, but make it not a business for him. 'Tis better it be a year later *before he can read,* than that he should this way get an aversion to learning. If you have any contest with him, let it be in matters of moment, of truth, and good nature; but lay no task on him about A B C. Use your skill to make his will supple and pliant to reason: teach him to love credit and commendation; to abhor being thought ill or meanly of, especially by you and his mother, and then the rest will come all easily. But I think if you will do that, you must not shackle and tie him up with rules about indifferent matters, nor rebuke him for every little fault, or perhaps some that to others would seem great ones; but of this I have said enough already.

156. When by these gentle ways he begins to *read,* some easy pleasant book, suited to his capacity, should be put into his hands, wherein the entertainment that he finds might draw him on, and reward his pains in reading, and yet not such as should fill his head with perfectly useless trumpery, or lay the principles of vice and folly. To this purpose, I think *Æsop's Fables* the best, which being stories apt to delight and entertain a child, may yet afford useful reflections to a grown man; and if his memory retain them all his life after, he will not repent to find them there, amongst his manly thoughts and serious business. If his *Æsop* has *pictures* in it, it will entertain him much the better, and encourage him to read, when it carries the increase of knowledge with it: for such visible objects children hear talked of in vain and without any satisfaction whilst they have no ideas of them; those ideas being not to be had from sounds, but from the things themselves or their pictures. And therefore I think as soon as he begins to spell, as many pictures of animals should be got him as can be found, with the printed names to them, which at the same time will invite him to read, and afford him matter of enquiry and knowledge. *Reynard the Fox* is another book I think may be made use of to the same purpose. And if those about him will talk to him often about the stories he has read, and hear him tell them, it will, besides other advantages, add encouragement and delight to his *reading,* when he finds there is some use and pleasure in it. These baits seem wholly neglected in the ordinary method; and 'tis usually long before learners find any use or pleasure in reading, which may tempt them to it, and so take books only for fashionable amusements, or impertinent troubles, good for nothing.

157. The Lord's Prayer, the Creeds, and Ten Commandments, 'tis necessary he should learn perfectly by heart; but, I think, not by reading them himself in his primer, but by somebody's repeating them to him, even before he can read. But learning by heart, and *learning to*

read, should not I think be mix'd, and so one made to clog the other. But his *learning to read* should be made as little trouble or business to him as might be.

What other books there are in *English* of the kind of those above-mentioned, fit to engage the liking of children, and tempt them to *read,* I do not know: but am apt to think, that children being generally delivered over to the method of schools, where the fear of the rod is to inforce, and not any pleasure of the employment to invite them to learn, this sort of useful books, amongst the number of silly ones that are of all sorts, have yet had the fate to be neglected; and nothing that I know has been considered of this kind out of the ordinary road of the horn-book, primer, psalter, Testament, and Bible.

158. As for the *Bible,* which children are usually employ'd in to exercise and improve their talent *in reading,* I think the promiscuous reading of it through by chapters as they lie in order, is so far from being of any advantage to children, either for the perfecting their *reading,* or principling their religion, that perhaps a worse could not be found. For what pleasure or encouragement can it be to a child to exercise himself in reading those parts of a book where he understands nothing? And how little are the law of *Moses,* the song of *Solomon,* the prophecies in the Old, and the Epistles and *Apocalypse* in the New Testament, suited to a child's capacity? And though the history of the Evangelists and the *Acts* have something easier, yet, taken altogether, it is very disproportional to the understanding of childhood. I grant that the principles of religion are to be drawn from thence, and in the words of the scripture; yet none should be propos'd to a child, but such as are suited to a child's capacity and notions. But 'tis far from this to read through *the whole Bible,* and that for reading's sake. And what an odd jumble of thoughts must a child have in his head, if he have any at all, such as he should have concerning religion, who in his tender age reads all the parts of the *Bible* indifferently as the word of God without any other distinction! I am apt to think, that this in some men has been the very reason why they never had clear and distinct thoughts of it all their lifetime.

159. And now I am by chance fallen on this subject, give me leave to say, that there are some parts of the *Scripture* which may be proper to be put into the hands of a child to engage him to read; such as are the story of *Joseph* and his brethren, of *David* and *Goliath,* of *David* and *Jonathan,* &c. and others that he should be made to read for his instruction, as that, *What you would have others do unto you, do you the same unto them;* and such other easy and plain moral rules, which being fitly chosen, might often be made use of, both for reading and instruction together; and so often read till they are throughly fixed in the memory; and then afterwards, as he grows ripe for them, may in their turns on fit occasions be inculcated as the standing and sacred rules of his life and actions. But the reading of the whole Scripture indifferently, is what I think very inconvenient for children, till after

having been made acquainted with the plainest fundamental parts of it, they have got some kind of general view of what they ought principally to believe and practise; which yet, I think, they ought to receive in the very words of the scripture, and not in such as men prepossess'd by systems and analogies are apt in this case to make use of and force upon them. Dr. *Worthington,* to avoid this, has made a catechism, which has all its answers in the precise words of the Scripture; a thing of good example, and such a sound form of words as no Christian can except against as not fit for his child to learn. Of this, as soon as he can say the Lord's Prayer, Creed, the Ten Commandments, by heart, it may be fit for him to learn a question every day, or every week, as his understanding is able to receive and his memory to retain them. And when he has this catechism perfectly by heart, so as readily and roundly to answer to any question in the whole book, it may be convenient to lodge in his mind the remaining moral rules scatter'd up and down in the Bible, as the best *exercise of his memory,* and that which may be always a rule to him, ready at hand, in the whole conduct of his life.

160. When he can read *English* well, it will be seasonable to enter him in *writing:* and here the first thing should be taught him is to *hold his pen right;* and this he should be perfect in before he should be suffered to put it to paper: For not only children but any body else that would do any thing well, should never be put upon too much of it at once, or be set to perfect themselves in two parts of an action at the same time, if they can possibly be separated. I think the Italian way of holding the pen between the thumb and the forefinger alone, may be best; but in this you may consult some good writing-master, or any other person who writes well and quick. When he has learn'd to hold his pen right, in the next place he should learn how to *lay his paper, and place his arm and body to it.* These practices being got over, the way to teach him to write without much trouble, is to get a plate graved with the characters of such a hand as you like best: but you must remember to have them a pretty deal bigger than he should ordinarily write; for every one naturally comes by degrees to write a less hand than he at first was taught, but never a bigger. Such a plate being graved, let several sheets of good writing-paper be printed off with red ink, which he has nothing to do but go over with a good pen fill'd with black ink, which will quickly bring his hand to the formation of those characters, being at first shewed where to begin, and how to form every letter. And when he can do that well, he must then exercise on fair paper; and so may easily be brought *to write* the hand you desire.

Sections 161–170

161. When he can write well and quick, I think it may be convenient not only to continue the exercise of his hand in writing, but also to improve the use of it farther in *drawing;* a thing very useful to a gentleman in several occasions; but especially if he travel, as that which helps a man often to express, in a few lines well put together, what a whole sheet of paper in writing would not be able to represent and make intelligible. How many buildings may a man see, how many machines and habits meet with, the ideas whereof would be easily retain'd and communicated by a little skill in *drawing;* which being committed to words, are in danger to be lost, or at best but ill retained in the most exact descriptions? I do not mean that I would have your son a *perfect painter;* to be that to any tolerable degree, will require more time than a young gentleman can spare from his other improvements of greater moment. But so much insight into *perspective* and skill in *drawing,* as will enable him to represent tolerably on paper any thing he sees, except faces, may, I think, be got in a little time, especially if he have a genius to it; but where that is wanting, unless it be in the things absolutely necessary, it is better to let him pass them by quietly, than to vex him about them to no purpose: and therefore in this, as in all other things not absolutely necessary, the rule holds, *nil invita Minerva.*

1. *Short-hand,* an art, as I have been told, known only in *England,* may perhaps be thought worth the learning, both for dispatch in what men write for their own memory, and concealment of what they would not have lie open to every eye. For he that has once learn'd any sort of character, may easily vary it to his own private use or fancy, and with more contraction suit it to the business he would employ it in. Mr. *Rich's,* the best contriv'd of any I have seen, may, as I think, by one who knows and considers grammar well, be made much easier and shorter. But for the learning this compendious way of writing, there will be no need hastily to look out a master; it will be early enough when any convenient opportunity offers itself at any time, after his hand is well settled in fair and quick writing. For boys have but little use of *short hand,* and should by no means practise it till they write perfectly well, and have throughly fixed the habit of doing so.

162. As soon as he can speak *English,* 'tis time for him to learn some other language. This no body doubts of, when *French* is propos'd. And the reason is, because people are accustomed to the right way of teaching that language, which is by talking it into children in constant conversation, and not by grammatical rules. The *Latin* tongue would

easily be taught the same way, if his tutor, being constantly with him, would talk nothing else to him, and make him answer still in the same language. But because *French* is a living language, and to be used more in speaking, that should be first learned, that the yet pliant organs of speech might be accustomed to a due formation of those sounds, and he get the habit of pronouncing *French* well, which is the harder to be done the longer it is delay'd.

163. When he can speak and read *French* well, which in this method is usually in a year or two, he should proceed to *Latin*, which 'tis a wonder parents, when they have had the experiment in *French*, should not think ought to be learned the same way, by talking and reading. Only care is to be taken whilst he is learning these foreign languages, by speaking and reading nothing else with his tutor, that he do not forget to read *English*, which may be preserved by his mother or some body else hearing him read some chosen parts of the scripture or other *English* book every day.

164. *Latin* I look upon as absolutely necessary to a gentleman; and indeed custom, which prevails over every thing, has made it so much a part of education, that even those children are whipp'd to it, and made spend many hours of their precious time uneasily in *Latin,* who after they are once gone from school, are never to have more to do with it as long as they live. Can there be any thing more ridiculous, than that a father should waste his own money and his son's time in setting him to learn the *Roman language,* when at the same time he designs him for a trade, wherein he having no use of *Latin,* fails not to forget that little which he brought from school, and which 'tis ten to one he abhors for the ill usage it procured him? Could it be believed, unless we had every where amongst us examples of it, that a child should be forced to learn the rudiments of a language which he is never to use in the course of life that he is designed to, and neglect all the while the writing a good hand and casting accounts, which are of great advantage in all conditions of life, and to most trades indispensably necessary? But though these qualifications, requisite to trade and commerce and the business of the world, are seldom or never to be had at grammar-schools, yet thither not only gentlemen send their younger sons, intended for trades, but even tradesmen and farmers fail not to send their children, though they have neither intention nor ability to make them scholars. If you ask them why they do this, they think it as strange a question as if you should ask them, why they go to church. Custom serves for reason, and has, to those who take it for reason, so consecrated this method, that it is almost religiously observed by them, and they stick to it, as if their children had scarce an orthodox education unless they learned *Lilly's* grammar.

165. But how necessary soever *Latin* be to some, and is thought to be to others to whom it is of no manner of use and service; yet the ordinary way of learning it in a grammar-school is that which having had thoughts about I cannot be forward to encourage. The reasons against it

128

are so evident and cogent, that they have prevailed with some intelligent persons to quit the ordinary road, not without success, though the method made use of was not exactly what I imagine the easiest, and in short is this. To trouble the child with no *grammar* at all, but to have *Latin,* as *English* has been, without the perplexity of rules, talked into him; for if you will consider it, *Latin* is no more unknown to a child, when he comes into the world, than *English:* and yet he learns *English* without master, rule, or grammar; and so might he *Latin* too, as *Tully* did, if he had some body always to talk to him in this language. And when we so often see a *French* woman teach an *English* girl to speak and read *French* perfectly in a year or two, without any rule of grammar, or any thing else but prattling to her, I cannot but wonder how gentlemen have overseen this way for their sons, and thought them more dull or incapable than their daughters.

166. If therefore a man could be got, who himself speaking good *Latin,* would always be about your son, talk constantly to him, and suffer him to speak or read nothing else, this would be the true and genuine way, and that which I would propose, not only as the easiest and best, wherein a child might, without pains or chiding, get a language, which others are wont to be whipt for at school six or seven years together: but also as that, wherein at the same time he might have his mind and manners formed, and he be instructed to boot in several sciences, such as are a good part of *geography, astronomy, chronology, anatomy,* besides some parts of *history,* and all other parts of knowledge of things that fall under the senses and require little more than memory. For there, if we would take the true way, our knowledge should begin, and in those things be laid the foundation; and not in the abstract notions of *logick* and *metaphysicks,* which are fitter to amuse than inform the understanding in its first setting out towards knowledge. When young men have had their heads employ'd a while in those abstract speculations without finding the success and improvement, or that use of them, which they expected, they are apt to have mean thoughts either of learning or themselves; they are tempted to quit their studies, and throw away their books as containing nothing but hard words and empty sounds; or else, to conclude, that if there be any real knowledge in them, they themselves have not understandings capable of it. That this is so, perhaps I could assure you upon my own experience. Amongst other things to be learned by a young gentleman in this method, whilst others of his age are wholly taken up with *Latin* and languages, I may also set down *geometry* for one; having known a young gentleman, bred something after this way, able to demonstrate several propositions in *Euclid* before he was thirteen.

167. But if such a man cannot be got, who speaks good *Latin,* and being able to instruct your son in all these parts of knowledge, will undertake it by this method; the next best is to have him taught as near this way as may be, which is by taking some easy and pleasant book, such as *Æsop's Fables,* and writing the *English* translation (made as literal as it can be) in one line, and the *Latin* words which answer each

of them, just over it in another. These let him read every day over and over again, till he perfectly understands the *Latin;* and then go on to another fable, till he be also perfect in that, not omitting what he is already perfect in, but sometimes reviewing that, to keep it in his memory. And when he comes to write, let these be set him for copies, which with the exercise of his hand will also advance him to *Latin.* This being a more imperfect way than by talking *Latin* unto him; the formation of the verbs first, and afterwards the declensions of the nouns and pronouns perfectly learned by heart, may facilitate his acquaintance with the genius and manner of the *Latin tongue,* which varies the signification of verbs and nouns, not as the modern languages do by particles prefix'd, but by changing the last syllables. More than this of grammar, It think he need not have, till he can read himself *Sanctii Minerva,* with *Scioppius* and *Perizonius's* notes.

In teaching of children, this too, I think, is to be observed, that in most cases where they stick, they are not to be farther puzzled by putting them upon finding it out themselves; as by asking such questions as these, (*viz.*) which is the nominative case, in the sentence they are to construe; or demanding what *aufero* signifies, to lead them to the knowledge what *abstlere* signifies, &c., when they cannot readily tell. This wastes time only in disturbing them; for whilst they are learning, and apply themselves with attention, they are to be kept in good humour, and every thing made easy to them, and as pleasant as possible. Therefore, wherever they are at a stand, and are willing to go forwards, help them presently over the difficulty, without any rebuke or chiding, remembering, that where harsher ways are taken, they are the effect only of pride and peevishness in the teacher, who expects children should instantly be masters of as much as he knows; whereas he should rather consider, that his business is to settle in them habits, not angrily to inculcate rules, which serve for little in the conduct of our lives; at least are of no use to children, who forget them as soon as given. In sciences where their reason is to be exercised, I will not deny but this method may sometimes be varied, and difficulties proposed on purpose to excite industry, and accustom the mind to employ its own strength and sagacity in reasoning. But yet, I guess, this is not to be done to children, whilst very young, nor at their entrance upon any sort of knowledge: then every thing of itself is difficult, and the great use and skill of a teacher is to make all as easy as he can: but particularly in learning of languages there is least occasion for posing of children. For languages being to be learned by rote, custom and memory, are then spoken in greatest perfection, when all rules of grammar are utterly forgotten. I grant the grammar of a language is sometimes very carefully to be studied, but it is not to be studied but by a grown man, when he applies himself to the understanding of any language critically, which is seldom the business of any but professed scholars. This I think will be agreed to, that if a gentleman be to study any language, it ought to be that of his own country, that he may understand the language which he has constant use of, with the utmost accuracy.

There is yet a further reason, why masters and teachers should raise no difficulties to their scholars; but on the contrary should smooth their way, and readily help them forwards, where they find them stop. Children's minds are narrow and weak, and usually susceptible but of one thought at once. Whatever is in a child's head, fills it for the time, especially if set on with any passion. It should therefore be the skill and art of the teacher to clear their heads of all other thoughts whilst they are learning of any thing, the better to make room for what he would instill into them, that it may be received with attention and application, without which it leaves no impression. The natural temper of children disposes their minds to wander. Novelty alone takes them; whatever that presents, they are presently eager to have a taste of, and are as soon satiated with it. They quickly grow weary of the same thing, and so have almost their whole delight in change and variety. It is a contradiction to the natural state of childhood for them to fix their fleeting thoughts. Whether this be owing to the temper of their brains, or the quickness or instability of their animal spirits, over which the mind has not yet got a full command; this is visible, that it is a pain to children to keep their thoughts steady to any thing. A lasting continued attention is one of the hardest tasks can be imposed on them; and therefore, he that requires their application, should endeavour to make what he proposes as grateful and agreeable as possible; at least he ought to take care not to join any displeasing or frightful idea with it. If they come not to their books with some kind of liking and relish, 'tis no wonder their thoughts should be perpetually shifting from what disgusts them; and seek better entertainment in more pleasing objects, after which they will unavoidably be gadding.

'Tis, I know, the usual method of tutors, to endeavour to procure attention in their scholars, and to fix their minds to the business in hand, by rebukes and corrections, if they find them ever so little wandering. But such treatment is sure to produce the quite contrary effect. Passionate words or blows from the tutor fill the child's mind with terror and affrightment, which immediately takes it wholly up, and leaves no room for other impressions. I believe there is nobody that reads this, but may recollect what disorder hasty or imperious words from his parents or teachers have caused in his thoughts; how for the time it has turned his brains, so that he scarce knew what was said by or to him. He presently lost the sight of what he was upon, his mind was filled with disorder and confusion, and in that state was no longer capable of attention to any thing else.

'Tis true, parents and governors ought to settle and establish their authority by an awe over the minds of those under their tuition; and to rule them by that: but when they have got an ascendant over them, they should use it with great moderation, and not make themselves such scare-crows that their scholars should always tremble in their sight. Such an austerity may make their government easy to themselves, but of very little use to their pupils. 'Tis impossible children should learn any thing whilst their thoughts are possessed and disturbed with any passion, especially fear, which makes the strongest impression on their yet tender and weak spirits. Keep the mind in an easy calm temper, when you would have it receive your instructions or any increase of knowledge. 'Tis as impossible to draw fair and regular characters on a trembling mind as on a shaking paper.

The great skill of a teacher is to get and keep the attention of his scholar; whilst he has that, he is sure to advance as fast as the learner's abilities will carry him; and without that, all his bustle and pother will be to little or no purpose. To attain this, he should make the child comprehend (as much as may be) the usefulness of what he teaches him, and let him see, by what he has learnt, that he can do something which he could not do before; something, which gives him some power and real advantage above others who are ignorant of it. To this he should add sweetness in all his instructions, and by a certain tenderness in his whole carriage, make the child sensible that he loves him and designs nothing but his good, the only way to beget love in the child, which will make him hearken to his lessons, and relish what he teaches him.

Nothing but obstinacy should meet with any imperiousness or rough usage. All other faults should be corrected with a gentle hand; and kind engaging words will work better and more effectually upon a willing mind, and even prevent a good deal of that perverseness which rough and imperious usage often produces in well disposed and generous minds. 'Tis true, obstinacy and wilful neglects must be mastered, even though it cost blows to do it: but I am apt to think perverseness in the pupils is often the effect of frowardness in the *tutor;* and that most children would seldom have deserved blows, if needless and misapplied roughness had not taught them ill-nature, and given them an aversion for their teacher and all that comes from him.

Inadvertency, forgetfulness, unsteadiness, and wandering of thought, are the natural faults of childhood; and therefore, where they are not observed to be wilful, are to be mention'd softly, and gain'd upon by time. If every slip of this kind produces anger and rating, the occasions of rebuke and corrections will return so often, that the tutor will be a constant terror and uneasiness to his pupils. Which one thing is enough to hinder their profiting by his lessons, and to defeat all his methods of instruction.

Let the awe he has got upon their minds be so tempered with the constant marks of tenderness and good will, that affection may spur them to their duty, and make them find a pleasure in complying with his dictates. This will bring them with satisfaction to their tutor; make them hearken to him, as to one who is their friend, that cherishes them, and takes pains for their good: this will keep their thoughts easy and free whilst they are with him, the only temper wherein the mind is capable of receiving new informations, and of admitting into itself those impressions, which, if not taken and retain'd, all that they and their teachers do together is lost labour; there is much uneasiness and little learning.

168. When by this way of interlining *Latin* and *English* one with another, he has got a moderate knowledge of the *Latin tongue,* he may then be advanced a little farther to the reading of some other easy *Latin*-book, such as *Justin* or *Eutropius;* and to make the reading and understanding of it the less tedious and difficult to him, let him help himself if he pleases with the *English* translation. Nor let the objection that he will then know it only by rote, fright any one. This, when well consider'd, is not of any moment against, but plainly for this way of learning a language. For languages are only to be learned by rote; and a man who does not speak *English* or *Latin* perfectly by rote, so that having thought of the thing he would speak of, his tongue of course, without thought of rule or grammar, falls into the proper expression and idiom of that language, does not speak it well, nor is master of it. And I would fain have any one name to me that tongue, that any one can learn, or speak as he should do, by the rules of grammar. Languages were made not by rules or art, but by accident, and the common use of the people. And he that will speak them well, has no other rule but that; nor any thing to trust to, but his memory, and the habit of speaking after the fashion learned from those, that are allowed to speak properly, which in other words is only to speak by rote.

It will possibly be asked here, is *grammar* then of no use? and have those who have taken so much pains in reducing several languages to rules and observations; who have writ so much about *declensions* and *conjugations,* about *concords* and *syntaxis,* lost their labour, and been learned to no purpose? I say not so; *grammar* has its place too. But this I think I may say, there is more stir a great deal made with it than there needs, and those are tormented about it, to whom it does not at all belong; I mean children, at the age wherein they are usually perplexed with it in grammar-schools.

There is nothing more evident, than that languages learnt by rote serve well enough for the common affairs of life and ordinary commerce. Nay, persons of quality of the softer sex, and such of them as have spent their time in well-bred company, shew us, that this plain natural way, without the least study or knowledge of *grammar,* can carry them to a great degree of elegancy and politeness in their language: and there are ladies who, without knowing what *tenses* and *participles, adverbs* and *prepositions* are, speak as properly and as correctly (they might take it for an ill compliment if I said as any country school-master) as most gentlemen who have been bred up in the ordinary methods of grammar-schools. Grammar therefore we see may be spared in some cases. The question then will be, to whom should it be taught, and when? To this I answer:

1. Men learn languages for the ordinary intercourse of society and communication of thoughts in common life, without any farther design

in the use of them. And for this purpose, the original way of learning a language by conversation not only serves well enough, but is to be preferred as the most expedite, proper and natural. Therefore, to this use of language one may answer, that grammar is not necessary. This so many of my readers must be forced to allow, as understand what I here say, and who conversing with others, understand them without having ever been taught the grammar of the *English* tongue. Which I suppose is the case of incomparably the greatest part of *English* men, of whom I have never yet known any one who learned his mother-tongue by rules.

2. Others there are, the greatest part of whose business in this world is to be done with their tongues and with their pens; and to these it is convenient, if not necessary, that they should speak properly and correctly, whereby they may let their thoughts into other men's minds the more easily, and with the greater impression. Upon this account it is, that any sort of speaking, so as will make him be understood, is not thought enough for a gentleman. He ought to study grammar amongst the other helps of speaking well, but it must be the grammar of his own tongue, of the language he uses, that he may understand his own country speech nicely, and speak it properly, without shocking the ears of those it is addressed to, with solecisms and offensive irregularities. And to this purpose grammar is necessary; but it is the grammar only of their own proper tongues, and to those only who would take pains in cultivating their language, and in perfecting their stiles. Whether all gentlemen should not do this, I leave to be considered, since the want of propriety and grammatical exactness is thought very misbecoming one of that rank, and usually draws on one guilty of such faults the censure of having had a lower breeding and worse company than suits with his quality. If this be so, (as I suppose it is) it will be matter of wonder why young gentlemen are forced to learn the grammars of foreign and dead languages, and are never once told of the grammar of their own tongues, they do not so much as know there is any such thing, much less is it made their business to be instructed in it. Nor is their own language ever proposed to them as worthy their care and cultivating, though they have daily use of it, and are not seldom, in the future course of their lives, judg'd of by their handsome or awkward way of expressing themselves in it. Whereas the languages whose grammars they have been so much employed in, are such as probably they shall scarce ever speak or write; or if, upon occasion, this should happen, they should be excused for the mistakes and faults they make in it. Would not a *Chinese* who took notice of this way of breeding, be apt to imagine that all our young gentlemen were designed to be teachers and professors of the dead languages of foreign countries, and not to be men of business in their own?

3. There is a third sort of men, who apply themselves to two or three foreign, dead, and (which amongst us are called the) learned languages, make them their study, and pique themselves upon their skill in them. No doubt, those who propose to themselves the learning of any

language with this view, and would be critically exact in it, ought carefully to study the grammar of it. I would not be mistaken here, as if this were to undervalue *Greek* and *Latin*. I grant these are languages of great use and excellency, and a man can have no place among the learned in this part of the world, who is a stranger to them. But the knowledge a gentleman would ordinarily draw for his use out of the *Roman* and *Greek* writers, I think he may attain without studying the grammars of those tongues, and by bare reading, may come to understand them sufficiently for all his purposes. How much farther he shall at any time be concerned to look into the grammar and critical niceties of either of these tongues, he himself will be able to determine when he comes to propose to himself the study of any thing that shall require it. Which brings me to the other part of the enquiry, *viz.*

When Grammar should be taught?

To which, upon the premised grounds, the answer is obvious, *viz.*

That if grammar ought to be taught at any time, it must be to one that can speak the language already; how else can he be taught the grammar of it? This at least is evident from the practice of the wise and learned nations amongst the antients. They made it a part of education to cultivate their own, not foreign tongues. The *Greeks* counted all other nations barbarous, and had a contempt for their languages. And tho' the *Greek* learning grew in credit amongst the *Romans,* towards the end of their commonwealth, yet it was the *Roman* tongue that was made the study of their youth: their own language they were to make use of, and therefore it was their own language they were instructed and exercised in.

But, more particularly to determine the proper season for grammar, I do not see how it can reasonably be made any one's study, but as an introduction to rhetorick; when it is thought time to put any one upon the care of polishing his tongue, and of speaking better than the illiterate, then is the time for him to be instructed in the rules of grammar, and not before. For grammar being to teach men not to speak, but to speak correctly and according to the exact rules of the tongue, which is one part of elegancy, there is little use of the one to him that has no need of the other; where rhetorick is not necessary, grammar may be spared. I know not why any one should waste his time, and beat his head about the *Latin* grammar, who does not intend to be a critick, or make speeches and write dispatches in it. When any one finds in himself a necessity or disposition to study any foreign language to the bottom, and to be nicely exact in the knowledge of it, it will be time enough to take a grammatical survey of it. If his use of it be only to understand some books writ in it, without a critical knowledge of the tongue itself, reading alone, as I have said, will attain this end, without charging the mind with the multiplied rules and intricacies of grammar.

169. For the exercise of his writing, let him sometimes translate *Latin* into *English:* but the learning of *Latin* being nothing but the learning of words, a very unpleasant business both to young and old, join as much other real knowledge with it as you can, beginning still with that which lies most obvious to the senses; such as is the knowledge of *minerals, plants* and *animals,* and particularly timber and fruit-trees, their parts, and ways of propagation, wherein a great deal may be taught a child which will not be useless to the man: but more especially *geography, astronomy,* and *anatomy.* But whatever you are teaching him, have a care still that you do not clog him with too much at once; or make anything his business but downright virtue, or reprove him for any thing but vice, or some apparent tendency to it.

170. But if after all his fate be to go to school to get the *Latin* tongue, 'twill be in vain to talk to you concerning the method I think best to be observ'd in schools; you must submit to that you find there, not expect to have it changed for your son; but yet by all means obtain, if you can, that he be not employed in making *Latin themes* and *declamations,* and least of all, *verses* of any kind. You may insist on it, if it will do any good, that you have no design to make him either a *Latin* orator or poet, but barely would have him understand perfectly a *Latin* author; and that you observe, those who teach any of the modern languages, and that with success, never amuse their scholars to make speeches or verses either in *French* or *Italian,* their business being language barely, and not invention.

Sections 171–180

171. But to tell you a little more fully why I would not have him exercised in making of *themes* and *verses*. 1. As to *themes,* they have, I confess, the pretence of something useful, which is to teach people to speak handsomely and well on any subject; which, if it could be attained this way, I own would be a great advantage, there being nothing more becoming a gentleman, nor more useful in all the occurrences of life, than to be able, on any occasion, to speak well and to the purpose. But this I say, that the making of *themes,* as is usual at schools, helps not one jot towards it: for do but consider what it is, in making a *theme,* that a young lad is employed about; it is to make a speech on some *Latin* saying; as *Omnia vincit amor;* or *Non licet in Bello bis peccare,* &c. And here the poor lad, who wants knowledge of those things he is to speak of, which is to be had only from time and observation, must set his invention on the rack, to say something where he knows nothing; which is a sort of *Egyptian* tyranny, to bid them make bricks who have not yet any of the materials. And therefore it is usual in such cases for the poor children to go to those of higher forms with this petition, *Pray give me a little sense;* which, whether it be more reasonable or more ridiculous, it is not easy to determine. Before a man can be in any capacity to speak on any subject, 'tis necessary he be acquainted with it; or else it is as foolish to set him to discourse of it, as to set a blind man to talk of colours, or a deaf man of musick. And would you not think him a little crack'd, who would require another to make an argument on a moot point, who understands nothing of our laws? And what, I pray, do school-boys understand concerning those matters which are used to be proposed to them in their *themes* as subjects to discourse on, to whet and exercise their fancies?

172. In the next place, consider the language that their *themes* are made in: 'tis *Latin,* a language foreign in their country, and long since dead every where: a language which your son, 'tis a thousand to one, shall never have an occasion once to make a speech in as long as he lives after he comes to be a man; and a language wherein the manner of expressing one's self is so far different from ours, that to be perfect in that would very little improve the purity and facility of his *English* stile. Besides that, there is now so little room or use for set speeches in our own language in any part of our *English* business, that I can see no pretence for this sort of exercise in our schools, unless it can be supposed, that the making of set *Latin* speeches should be the way to teach men to speak well in *English extempore.* The way to that, I should think rather to be this: that there should be propos'd to young

137

gentlemen rational and useful questions, suited to their age and capacities, and on subjects not wholly unknown to them nor out of their way: such as these, when they are ripe for exercises of this nature, they should *extempore,* or after a little meditation upon the spot, speak to, without penning of any thing: for I ask, if we will examine the effects of this way of learning to speak well, who speak best in any business, when occasion calls them to it upon any debate, either those who have accustomed themselves to compose and write down beforehand what they would say; or those, who thinking only of the matter, to understand that as well as they can, use themselves only to speak *extempore?* And he that shall judge by this, will be little apt to think, that the accustoming him to studied speeches and set compositions, is the way to fit a young gentleman for business.

173. But perhaps we shall be told, 'tis to improve and perfect them in the *Latin* tongue. 'Tis true, that is their proper business at school; but the making of *themes* is not the way to it: that perplexes their brains about invention of things to be said, not about the signification of words to be learn'd; and when they are making a *theme,* 'tis thoughts they search and sweat for, and not language. But the learning and mastery of a tongue being uneasy and unpleasant enough in itself, should not be cumbred with any other difficulties, as is done in this way of proceeding. In fine, if boys' invention be to be quicken'd by such exercise, let them make *themes* in *English,* where they have facility and a command of words, and will better see what kind of thoughts they have, when put into their own language. And if the *Latin* tongue be to be learned, let it be done the easiest way, without toiling and disgusting the mind by so uneasy an employment as that of making speeches joined to it.

174. If these may be any reasons against children's making *Latin* themes at school, I have much more to say, and of more weight, against their making *verses;* verses of any sort: for if he has no *genius* to *poetry,* 'tis the most unreasonable thing in the world to torment a child and waste his time about that which can never succeed; and if he have a poetick vein, 'tis to me the strangest thing in the world that the father should desire or suffer it to be cherished or improved. Methinks the parents should labour to have it stifled and suppressed as much as may be; and I know not what reason a father can have to wish his son a poet, who does not desire to have him bid defiance to all other callings and business; which is not yet the worst of the case; for if he proves a successful rhymer, and gets once the reputation of a wit, I desire it may be considered what company and places he is like to spend his time in, nay, and estate too: for it is very seldom seen, that any one discovers mines of gold or silver in *Parnassus.* 'Tis a pleasant air, but a barren soil; and there are very few instances of those who have added to their patrimony by any thing they have reaped from thence. Poetry and gaming, which usually go together, are alike in this too, that they seldom bring any advantage but to those who have nothing else to live on. Men of estates almost constantly go away losers; and 'tis well if they escape at a cheaper rate than their whole estates, or the greatest part

of them. If therefore you would not have your son the fiddle to every jovial company, without whom the sparks could not relish their wine nor know how to pass an afternoon idly; if you would not have him to waste his time and estate to divert others, and contemn the dirty acres left him by his ancestors, I do not think you will much care he should be a *poet*, or that his school-master should enter him in versifying. But yet, if any one will think poetry a desirable quality in his son, and that the study of it would raise his fancy and parts, he must needs yet confess, that to that end reading the excellent *Greek* and *Roman* poets is of more use than making bad verses of his own, in a language that is not his own. And he whose design it is to excel in *English* poetry, would not, I guess, think the way to it were to make his first essays in *Latin* verses.

175. Another thing very ordinary in the vulgar method of grammar-schools there is, of which I see no use at all, unless it be to baulk young lads in the way to learning languages, which, in my opinion, should be made as easy and pleasant as may be; and that which was painful in it, as much as possible quite removed. That which I mean, and here complain of, is, their being to learn by heart, great parcels of the authors which are taught them; wherein I can discover no advantage at all, especially to the business they are upon. Languages are to be learned only by reading and talking, and not by scraps of authors got by heart; which when a man's head is stuffed with, he has got the just furniture of a pedant, and 'tis the ready way to make him one; than which there is nothing less becoming a gentleman. For what can be more ridiculous, than to mix the rich and handsome thoughts and sayings of others with a deal of poor stuff of his own; which is thereby the more exposed, and has no other grace in it, nor will otherwise recommend the speaker, than a thread-bare russet coat would, that was set off with large patches of scarlet and glittering brocade. Indeed, where a passage comes in the way, whose matter is worth remembrance, and the expression of it very close and excellent, (as there are many such in the antient authors) it may not be amiss to lodge it in the mind of young scholars, and with such admirable strokes of those great masters sometimes exercise the memories of school-boys. But their learning of their lessons by heart, as they happen to fall out in their books, without choice or distinction, I know not what it serves for, but no misspend their time and pains, and give them a disgust and aversion to their books, wherein they find nothing but useless trouble.

176. I hear it is said, that children should be employ'd in getting things by heart, to exercise and improve their memories. I could wish this were said with as much authority of reason, as it is with forwardness of assurance, and that this practice were established upon good observation more than old custom; for it is evident, that strength of memory is owing to an happy constitution, and not to any habitual improvement got by exercise. 'Tis true, what the mind is intent upon, and, for fear of letting it slip, often imprints afresh on itself by frequent reflection, that it is apt to retain, but still according to its own natural

strength of retention. An impression made on bees-wax or lead, will not last so long as on brass or steel. Indeed, if it be renew'd often, it may last the longer; but every new reflecting on it is a new impression; and 'tis from thence one is to reckon, if one would know how long the mind retains it. But the learning pages of *Latin* by heart, no more fits the memory for retention of any thing else, than the graving of one sentence in lead makes it the more capable of retaining firmly any other characters. If such a sort of exercise of the memory were able to give it strength, and improve our parts, players of all other people must needs have the best memories and be the best company. But whether the scraps they have got into their heads this way, make them remember other things the better; and whether their parts be improved proportionably to the pains they have taken in getting by heart others' sayings, experience will shew. Memory is so necessary to all parts and conditions of life, and so little is to be done without it, that we are not to fear it should grow dull and useless for want of exercise, if exercise would make it grow stronger. But I fear this faculty of the mind is not capable of much help and amendment in general by any exercise or endeavour of ours, at least not by that used upon this pretence in grammar-schools. And if *Xerxes* was able to call every common soldier by name in his army that consisted of no less than an hundred thousand men, I think it may be guessed, he got not this wonderful ability by learning his lessons by heart when he was a boy. This method of exercising and improving the memory by toilsome repetitions without book of what they read, is, I think, little used in the education of princes, which if it had that advantage is talked of, should be as little neglected in them as in the meanest school-boys: princes having as much need of good memories as any men living, and have generally an equal share in this faculty with other men; though it has never been taken care of this way. What the mind is intent upon and careful of, that it remembers best, and for the reason above-mentioned: to which, if method and order be joined, all is done, I think, that can be, for the help of a weak memory; and he that will take any other way to do it, especially that of charging it with a train of other peoples' words, which he that learns cares not for, will, I guess, scarce find the profit answer half the time and pains employ'd in it.

I do not mean hereby, that there should be no exercise given to children's memories. I think their memories should be employ'd, but not in learning by rote whole pages out of books, which, the lesson being once said, and that task over, are delivered up again to oblivion and neglected for ever. This mends neither the memory nor the mind. What they should learn by heart out of authors, I have above mentioned: and such wise and useful sentences being once being once given in charge to their memories, they should never be suffer'd to forget again, but be often called to account for them: whereby, besides the use those sayings may be to them in their future life, as so many good rules and observations, they will be taught to reflect often, and bethink themselves what they have to remember, which is the only way to make the memory quick and useful. The custom of frequent reflection will keep their minds from running adrift, and call their thoughts home from useless unattentive roving: and therefore I think it may do well, to give them something every day to remember, but something still, that is in itself worth the remembering, and what you would never have out of mind, whenever you call, or they themselves search for it. This will oblige them often to turn their thoughts inwards, than which you cannot wish them a better intellectual habit.

177. But under whose care soever a child is put to be taught during the tender and flexible years of his life, this is certain, it should be one who thinks *Latin* and *language* the least part of education; one who knowing how much virtue and a well-temper'd soul is to be preferred to any sort of *learning* or *language,* makes it his chief business to form the mind of his scholars, and give that a right disposition; which if once got, though all the rest should be neglected, would in due time produce all the rest; and which, if it be not got and settled so as to keep out ill and vicious habits, *languages* and *sciences* and all the other accomplishments of education, will be to no purpose but to make the worse or more dangerous man. And indeed whatever stir there is made about getting of *Latin* as the great and difficult business, his mother may teach it him herself, if she will but spend two or three hours in a day with him, and make him read the Evangelists in *Latin* to her: for she need but buy a *Latin* Testament, and having got some body to mark the last syllable but one where it is long in words above two syllables, (which is enough to regulate her pronunciation, and accenting the words) read daily in the *Gospels,* and then let her avoid understanding them in *Latin* if she can. And when she understands the Evangelists in *Latin,* let her, in the same manner, read *Æsop's* Fables, and so proceed on to *Eutropius, Justin,* and other such books. I do not mention this, as an imagination of what I fancy may do, but as of a thing I have known done, and the *Latin* tongue with ease got this way.

But, to return to what I was saying: he that takes on him the charge of bringing up young men, especially young gentlemen, should have something more in him than *Latin,* more than even a knowledge in the liberal sciences: he should be a person of eminent virtue and prudence, and with good sense, have good humour, and the skill to carry himself with gravity, ease and kindness, in a constant conversation with his pupils. But of this I have spoken at large in another place.

178. At the same time that he is learning *French* and *Latin,* a child, as has been said, may also be enter'd in *Arithmetick, Geography, Chronology, History* and *Geometry* too. For if these be taught him in *French* or *Latin,* when he begins once to understand either of these tongues, he will get a knowledge in these sciences, and the language to boot.

Geography I think should be begun with: for the learning of the figure of the *globe,* the situation and boundaries of the four parts of the world, and that of particular kingdoms and countries, being only an exercise of the eyes and memory, a child with pleasure will learn and retain them. And this is so certain, that I now live in the house with a child whom his mother has so well instructed this way in *geography,* that he knew the limits of the four parts of the world, could readily point, being ask'd, to any country upon the globe, or any county in the map of *England;* knew all the great rivers, promontories, straits and bays in the world, and could find the longitude and latitude of any place, before he was six years old. These things, that he will thus learn by sight, and have by rote in his memory, are not all, I confess, that he is to learn upon the *globes.* But yet it is a good step and preparation to it, and will make the remainder much easier, when his judgment is grown ripe enough for it: besides that, it gets so much time now; and by the pleasure of knowing things, leads him on insensibly to the gaining of languages.

179. When he has the natural parts of the globe well fix'd in his memory, it may then be time to begin *arithmetick.* By the natural parts of the globe, I mean the several positions of the parts of the earth and sea, under different names and distinctions of countries, not coming yet to those artificial and imaginary lines which have been invented, and are only suppos'd for the better improvement of that science.

180. *Arithmetick* is the easiest, and consequently the first sort of abstract reasoning, which the mind commonly bears or accustoms itself to: and is of so general use in all parts of life and business, that scarce any thing is to be done without it. This is certain, a man cannot have too much of it, nor too perfectly: he should therefore begin to be exercis'd in *counting,* as soon, and as far, as he is capable of it; and do something in it every day, till he is master of the art of *numbers.* When he understands *addition* and *subtraction,* he then may be advanced farther in *geography,* after he is acquainted with the *poles, zones, parallel circles,* and *meridians,* be taught *longitude* and *latitude,* and by them be made to understand the use of maps, and by the numbers placed on their sides, to know the respective situation of countries, and how to find them out on the terrestrial globe. Which when he can readily do, he may then be entered in the celestial; and there going over all the circles again, with a more particular observation of the Ecliptick, or Zodiack, to fix them all very clearly and distinctly in his mind, he may be taught the figure and position of the several constellations, which may be shewed him first upon the globe, and then in the heavens.

When that is done, and he knows pretty well the constellations of this our hemisphere, it may be time to give him some notions of this our planetary world; and to that purpose, it may not be amiss to make him a draught of the *Copernican* system, and therein explain to him the situation of the planets, their respective distances from the sun, the centre of their revolutions. This will prepare him to understand the motion and theory of the planets, the most easy and natural way. For since astronomers no longer doubt of the motion of the planets about the sun, it is fit he should proceed upon that hypothesis, which is not only the simplest and least perplexed for a learner, but also the likeliest to be true in itself. But in this, as in all other parts of instruction, great care must be taken with children, to begin with that which is plain and simple, and to teach them as little as can be at once, and settle that well in their heads before you proceed to the next, or any thing new in that science. Give them first one simple idea, and see that they take it right, and perfectly comprehend it before you go any farther, and then add some other simple idea which lies next in your way to what you aim at; and so proceeding by gentle and insensible steps, children without confusion and amazement will have their understandings opened and their thoughts extended farther than could have been expected. And when any one has learn'd any thing himself, there is no such way to fix it in his memory, and to encourage him to go on, as to set him to teach it others.

Sections 181-190

181. When he has once got such an acquaintance with the globes, as is above mentioned, he may be fit to be tried in a little *geometry;* wherein I think the first six books of *Euclid* enough for him to be taught. For I am in some doubt, whether more to a man of business be necessary or useful. At least, if he have a genius and inclination to it, being enter'd so far by his tutor, he will be able to go on of himself without a teacher.

The *globes* therefore must be studied, and that diligently; and I think may be begun betimes, if the tutor will be but careful to distinguish what the child is capable of knowing, and what not; for which this may be a rule that perhaps will go a pretty way, *viz.* that children may be taught anything that falls under their senses, especially their sight, as far as their memories only are exercised: and thus a child very young may learn, which is the *Æquator,* which the *Meridian,* &c. which *Europe,* and which *England,* upon the globes, as soon almost as he knows the rooms of the house he lives in, if care be taken not to teach him too much at once, nor to set him upon a new part, till that which he is upon be perfectly learned and fixed in his memory.

182. With geography, *chronology* ought to go hand in hand. I mean the general part of it, so that he may have in his mind a view of the whole current of time, and the several considerable *epochs* that are made use of in history. Without these two, history, which is the great mistress of prudence and civil knowledge, and ought to be the proper study of a gentleman, or man of business in the world; without geography and *chronology,* I say, history will be very ill retain'd, and very little useful; but be only a jumble of matters of fact, confusedly heaped together without order or instruction. 'Tis by these two that the actions of mankind are ranked into their proper places of time and countries, under which circumstances they are not only much easier kept in the memory, but in that natural order, are only capable to afford those observations which make a man the better and the abler for reading them.

183. When I speak of *chronology* as a science he should be perfect in, I do not mean the little controversies that are in it. These are endless, and most of them of so little importance to a gentleman, as not to deserve to be enquir'd into, were they capable of an easy decision. And therefore all that learned noise and dust of the chronologist is wholly to be avoided. The most useful book I have seen in that part of learning, is

a small treatise of *Strauchius,* which is printed in twelves, under the title of *Breviarium Chronologicum,* out of which may be selected all that is necessary to be taught a young gentleman concerning *chronology;* for all that is in that treatise a learner need not be cumbred with. He has in him the most remarkable or useful *epochs* reduced all to that of the *Julian Period,* which is the easiest and plainest and surest method that can be made use of in *chronology.* To this treatise of *Strauchius, Helvicus's* tables may be added, as a book to be turned to on all occasions.

184. As nothing teaches, so nothing delights more than history. The first of these recommends it to the study of grown men, the latter makes me think it the fittest for a young lad, who as soon as he is instructed in chronology, and acquainted with the several *epochs* in use in this part of the world, and can reduce them to the *Julian Period,* should then have some *Latin history* put into his hand. The choice should be directed by the easiness of the stile; for wherever he begins, chronology will keep it from confusion; and the pleasantness of the subject inviting him to read, the language will insensibly be got without that terrible vexation and uneasiness which children suffer where they are put into books beyond their capacity; such as are the *Roman* orators and poets, only to learn the *Roman* language. When he has by reading master'd the easier, such perhaps as *Justin, Eutropius, Quintius Curtius, &c.* the next degree to these will give him no great trouble: and thus by a gradual progress from the plaintest and easiest *historians,* he may at last come to read the most difficult and sublime of the *Latin* authors, such as are *Tully, Virgil,* and *Horace.*

185. The knowledge of *virtue,* all along from the beginning, in all the instances he is capable of, being taught him more by practice than rules; and the love of reputation, instead of satisfying his appetite, being made habitual in him, I know not whether he should read any other discourses of morality but what he finds in the Bible; or have any system of *ethicks* put into his hand till he can read *Tully's Offices* not as a school-boy to learn *Latin,* but as one that would be informed in the principles and precepts of virtue for the conduct of his life.

186. When he has pretty well digested *Tully's Offices,* and added to it, *Puffendorf de Officio Hominis & Civis,* it may be seasonable to set him upon *Grotius de Jure Belli & Pacis,* or, which perhaps is the better of the two, *Puffendorf de Jure naturali & Gentium;* wherein he will be instructed in the natural rights of men, and the original and foundations of society, and the duties resulting from thence. This *general part of civil-law* and history, are studies which a gentleman should not barely touch at, but constantly dwell upon, and never have done with. A virtuous and well-behaved young man, that is well-versed in the *general part of the civil-law* (which concerns not the chicane of private cases, but the affairs and intercourse of civilized nations in general, grounded upon principles of reason) understands *Latin* well, and can write a good

hand, one may turn loose into the world with great assurance that he will find employment and esteem every where.

187. It would be strange to suppose an *English* gentleman should be ignorant of the *law* of his country. This, whatever station he is in, is so requisite, that from a Justice of the Peace to a Minister of State I know no place he can well fill without it. I do not mean the chicane or wrangling and captious part of the law: a gentleman, whose business is to seek the true measures of right and wrong, and not the arts how to avoid doing the one, and secure himself in doing the other, ought to be as far from such a study of the *law,* as he is concerned diligently to apply himself to that wherein he may be serviceable to his country. And to that purpose, I think the right way for a gentleman to study *our law,* which he does not design for his calling, is to take a view of our *English* constitution and government in the antient books of the *common-law,* and some more modern writers, who out of them have given an account of this government. And having got a true idea of that, then to read our history, and with it join in every king's reign the *laws* then made. This will give an insight into the reason of our *statutes,* and shew the true ground upon which they came to be made, and what weight they ought to have.

188. *Rhetorick* and *logick* being the arts that in the ordinary method usually follow immediately after grammar, it may perhaps be wondered that I have said to little of them. The reason is, because of the little advantage young people receive by them: for I have seldom or never observed any one to get the skill of reasoning well, or speaking handsomely, by studying those rules which pretend to reach it: and therefore I would have a young gentleman take a view of them in the shortest systems could be found, without dwelling long on the contemplation and study of those formalities. Right reasoning is founded on something else than the *predicaments* and *predicables,* and does not consist in talking in *mode* and *figure* it self. But 'tis beside my present business to enlarge upon this speculation. To come therefore to what we have in hand; if you would have your son *reason well,* let him read *Chillingworth;* and if you would have him speak well, let him be conversant in *Tully,* to give him the true *idea* of *eloquence;* and let him read those things that are well writ in *English,* to perfect his style in the purity of our language.

189. If the use and end of right reasoning be to have right notions and a right judgment of things, to distinguish betwixt truth and falsehood, right and wrong, and to act accordingly; be sure not to let your son be bred up in the art and formality of disputing, either practising it himself, or admiring it in others; unless instead of an able man, you desire to have him an insignificant wrangler, opiniator in discourse, and priding himself in contradicting others; or, which is worse, questioning every thing, and thinking there is no such thing as truth to be sought, but only victory, in disputing. There cannot be any thing so disingenuous, so misbecoming a gentleman or any one who

pretends to be a rational creature, as not to yield to plain reason and the conviction of clear arguments. Is there any thing more consistent with civil conversation, and the end of all debate, than not to take an answer, though never so full and satisfactory, but still to go on with the dispute as long as equivocal sounds can furnish (a *medius terminus*) a term to wrangle with on the one side, or a distinction on the other; whether pertinent or impertinent, sense or nonsense, agreeing with or contrary to what he had said before, it matters not. For this, in short, is the way and perfection of logical disputes, that the opponent never takes any answer, nor the respondent ever yields to any argument. This neither of them must do, whatever becomes of truth or knowledge, unless he will pass for a poor baffled wretch, and lie under the disgrace of not being able to maintain whatever he has once affirm'd, which is the great aim and glory in disputing. Truth is to be found and supported by a mature and due consideration of things themselves, and not by artificial terms and ways of arguing: these lead not men so much into the discovery of truth, as into a captious and fallacious use of doubtful words, which is the most useless and most offensive way of talking, and such as least suits a gentleman or a lover of truth of any thing in the world.

There can scarce be a greater defect in a gentleman than not to express himself well either in writing or speaking. But yet I think I may ask my reader, whether he doth not know a great many, who live upon their estates, and so with the name should have the qualities of gentlemen, who cannot so much as tell a story as they should, much less speak clearly and persuasively in any business. This I think not to be so much their fault, as the fault of their education; for I must, without partiality, do my countrymen this right, that where they apply themselves, I see none of their neighbours outgo them. They have been taught *rhetorick,* but yet never taught how to express themselves handsomely with their tongues or pens in the language they are always to use; as if the names of the figures that embellish'd the discourses of those who understood the art of speaking, were the very art and skill of speaking well. This, as all other things of practice, is to be learn'd not by a few or a great many rules given, but by exercise and application according to good rules, or rather patterns, till habits are got, and a facility of doing it well.

Agreeable hereunto, perhaps it might not be amiss to make children, as soon as they are capable of it, often to tell a story of any thing they know; and to correct at first the most remarkable fault they are guilty of in their way putting it together. When that fault is cured, then to shew them the next, and so on, till one after another, all, at least the gross ones, are mended. When they can tell tales pretty well, then it may be the time to make them write them. The Fables of *Æsop,* the only book almost that I know fit for children, may afford them matter for this exercise of writing *English,* as well as for reading and translating, to enter them in the *Latin* tongue. When they have got past the faults of grammar, and can join in a continued coherent discourse the several

148

parts of a story, without bald and unhandsome forms of transition (as is usual) often repeated, he that desires to perfect them yet farther in this, which is the first step to speaking well and needs no invention, may have recourse to *Tully,* and by putting in practice those rules which that master of eloquence gives in his first book *de inventione,*

20, make them know wherein the skill and graces of an handsome narrative, according to the several subjects and designs of it, lie. Of each of which rules fit examples may be found out, and therein they may be shewn how others have practised them. The antient classick authors afford plenty of such examples, which they should be made not only to translate, but have set before them as patterns for their daily imitation.

When they understand how to write *English* with due connexion, propriety and order, and are pretty well masters of a tolerable narrative style, they may be advanced to writing of letters; wherein they should not be put upon any strains of wit or compliment, but taught to express their own plain easy sense, without any incoherence, confusion or roughness. And when they are perfect in this, they may, to raise their thoughts, have set before them the examples of *Voitures,* for the entertainment of their friends at a distance, with letters of compliment, mirth, raillery or diversion; and *Tully's Epistles,* as the best pattern whether for business or conversation. The writing of letters has so much to do in all the occurrences of human life, that no gentleman can avoid shewing himself in this kind of writing. Occasions will daily force him to make this use of his pen, which, besides the consequences that, in his affairs, his well or ill managing of it often draws after it, always lays him open to a severer examination of his breeding, sense, and abilities, than oral discourses; whose transient faults dying for the most part with the sound that gives them life, and so not subject to a strict review, more easily escape observation and censure.

Had the methods of education been directed to their right end, one would have thought this so necessary a part could not have been neglected whilst themes and verses in *Latin,* of no use at all, were so constantly every where pressed, to the racking of children's inventions beyond their strength and hindering their chearful progress in learning the tongues by unnatural difficulties. But custom has so ordain'd it, and who dares disobey? And would it not be very unreasonable to require of a learned country school-master (who has all the tropes and figures in *Farnaby's Rhetorick* at his fingers' ends) to teach his scholar to express himself handsomely in *English,* when it appears to be so little his business or thought, that the boy's mother (despised, 'tis like, as illiterate for not having read a system of *logick* and *rhetorick*) outdoes him in it?

To write and speak correctly gives a grace and gains a favourable attention to what one has to say: and since 'tis *English* that an *English* gentleman will have constant use of, that is the language he should

149

chiefly cultivate, and wherein most care should be taken to polish and perfect his style. To speak or write better *Latin* than *English,* may make a man be talk'd of, but he would find it more to his purpose to express himself well in his own tongue, that he uses every moment, than to have the vain commendation of others for a very insignificant quality. This I find universally neglected, and no care taken any where to improve young men in their own language, that they may thoroughly understand and be masters of it. If any one among us have a facility or purity more than ordinary in his mother tongue, it is owing to chance, or his genius, or any thing rather than to his education or any care of his teacher. To mind what *English* his pupil speaks or writes, is below the dignity of one bred up amongst *Greek* and *Latin,* though he have but little of them himself. These are the learned languages fit only for learned men to meddle with and teach; *English* is the language of the illiterate vulgar: tho' yet we see the polity of some of our neighbours hath not thought it beneath the publick care to promote and reward the improvement of their own language. Polishing and enriching their tongue is no small business amongst them; it hath colleges and stipends appointed it, and there is raised amongst them a great ambition and emulation of writing correctly: and we see what they are come to by it, and how far they have spread one of the worst languages possibly in this part of the world, if we look upon it as it was in some few reigns backwards, whatever it be now. The great men among the *Romans* were daily exercising themselves in their own language; and we find yet upon record the names of orators, who taught some of their emperors *Latin,* though it were their mother tongue.

'Tis plain the *Greeks* were yet more nice in theirs. All other speech was barbarous to them but their own, and no foreign language appears to have been studied or valued amongst that learned and acute people; tho' it be past doubt that they borrowed their learning and philosophy from abroad.

I am not here speaking against *Greek* and *Latin;* I think they ought to be studied, and the *Latin* at least understood well by every gentleman. But whatever foreign languages a young man meddles with (and the more he knows the better) that which he should critically study, and labour to get a facility, clearness and elegancy to express himself in, should be his own; and to this purpose he should daily be exercised in it.

190. *Natural philosophy,* as a speculative science, I imagine we have none, and perhaps I may think I have reason to say we never shall be able to make a science of it. The works of nature are contrived by a wisdom, and operate by ways too far surpassing our faculties to discover or capacities to conceive, for us ever to be able to reduce them into a science. *Natural philosophy* being the knowledge of the principles, properties and operations of things as they are in themselves, I imagine there are two parts of it, one comprehending *spirits,* with their nature and qualities, and the other *bodies.* The first of these is usually referred

to *metaphysicks:* but under what title soever the consideration of *spirits* comes, I think it ought to go before the study of matter and body, not as a science that can be methodized into a system, and treated of upon principles of knowledge; but as an enlargement of our minds towards a truer and fuller comprehension of the intellectual world to which we are led both by reason and revelation. And since the clearest and largest discoveries we have of other *spirits,* besides God and our own souls, is imparted to us from heaven by revelation, I think the information that at least young people should have of them, should be taken from that revelation. To this purpose, I conclude, it would be well, if there were made a good history of the Bible, for young people to read; wherein if every thing that is fit to be put into it, were laid down in its due order of time, and several things omitted which are suited only to riper age, that confusion which is usually produced by promiscuous reading of the Scripture, as it lies now bound up in our Bibles, would be avoided. And also this other good obtained, that by reading of it constantly, there would be instilled into the minds of children a notion and belief of *spirits,* they having so much to do in all the transactions of that history, which will be a good preparation to the study of *bodies.* For without the notion and allowance of *spirit,* our philosophy will be lame and defective in one main part of it, when it leaves out the contemplation of the most excellent and powerful part of the creation.

Sections 191–200

191. Of this *History of the Bible,* I think too it would be well if there were a short and plain epitome made, containing the chief and most material heads, for children to be conversant in as soon as they can read. This, though it will lead them early into some notion of *spirits,* yet it is not contrary to what I said above, that I would not have children troubled, whilst young, with notions of *spirits;* whereby my meaning was, that I think it inconvenient that their yet tender minds should receive early impressions of *goblins, spectres,* and *apparitions,* wherewith their maids and those about them are apt to fright them into a compliance with their orders, which often proves a great inconvenience to them all their lives after, by subjecting their minds to frights, fearful apprehensions, weakness and superstition; which when coming abroad into the world and conversation they grow weary and ashamed of, it not seldom happens, that to make, as they think, a thorough cure, and ease themselves of a load which has sat so heavy on them, they throw away the thoughts of all *spirits* together, and so run into the other, but worse, extream.

192. The reason why I would have this premised to the *study of bodies,* and the Doctrine of the Scriptures well imbibed before young men be entered in *natural philosophy,* is, because matter, being a thing that all our senses are constantly conversant with, it is so apt to possess the mind, and exclude all other beings but matter, that prejudice, grounded on such principles, often leaves no room for the admittance of spirits, or the allowing any such things as *immaterial beings in rerum natura;* when yet it is evident that by mere matter and motion none of the great phaenomena of nature can be resolved, to instance but in that common one of gravity, which I think impossible to be explained by any natural operation of matter, or any other law of motion, but the positive will of a superior being so ordering it. And therefore since the deluge cannot be well explained without admitting something out of the ordinary course of nature, I propose it to be considered whether God's altering the centre of gravity in the earth for a time (a thing as intelligible as gravity it self, which perhaps a little variation of causes unknown to us would produce) will not more easily account for *Noah's* flood than any hypothesis yet made use of to solve it. I hear the great objection to this, is, that it would produce but a partial deluge. But the alteration of the centre of gravity once allowed, 'tis no hard matter to conceive that the divine power might make the centre of gravity, plac'd at a due distance from the centre of the earth, move round it in a convenient space of time, whereby the flood would become universal,

and, as I think, answer all the phaenomena of the deluge as delivered by *Moses,* at an easier rate than those many hard suppositions that are made use of to explain it. But this is not a place for that argument, which is here only mentioned by the bye, to shew the necessity of having recourse to something beyond bare matter and its motion in the explication of nature; to which the notions of spirits and their power, as delivered in the Bible, where so much is attributed to their operation, may be a fit preparative, reserving to a fitter opportunity a fuller explication of this hypothesis, and the application of it to all the parts of the deluge, and any difficulties can be supposed in the history of the flood, as recorded in the scripture.

193. But to return to the study of *natural philosophy.* Tho' the world be full of systems of it, yet I cannot say, I know any one which can be taught a young man as a science wherein he may be sure to find truth and certainty, which is what all sciences give an expectation of. I do not hence conclude, that none of them are to be read. It is necessary for a gentleman in this learned age to look into some of them to fit himself for conversation: but whether that of *Des Cartes* be put into his hands, as that which is most in fashion, or it be thought fit to give him a short view of that and several others also, I think the systems of *natural philosophy* that have obtained in this part of the world, are to be read more to know the *hypotheses,* and to understand the terms and ways of talking of the several sects, than with hopes to gain thereby a comprehensive, scientifical and satisfactory knowledge of the works of nature. Only this may be said, that the modern *Corpuscularians* talk in most things more intelligibly than the *Peripateticks,* who possessed the schools immediately before them. He that would look further back, and acquaint himself with the several opinions of the antients, may consult Dr. *Cudworth's Intellectual System,* wherein that very learned author hath with such accurateness and judgment collected and explained the opinions of the *Greek* philosophers, that what principles they built on, and what were the chief *hypotheses* that divided them, is better to be seen in him than any where else that I know. But I would not deter any one from the study of nature because all the knowledge we have or possibly can have of it cannot be brought into a science. There are very many things in it that are convenient and necessary to be known to a gentleman; and a great many other that will abundantly reward the pains of the curious with delight and advantage. But these, I think, are rather to be found amongst such writers as have employed themselves in making rational experiments and observations than in starting barely speculative systems. Such writings therefore, as many of Mr. *Boyle's* are, with others that have writ of *husbandry, planting, gardening,* and the like, may be fit for a gentleman, when he has a little acquainted himself with some of the systems of the *natural philosophy* in fashion.

194. Though the systems of *physicks* that I have met with, afford little encouragement to look for certainty or science in any treatise which shall pretend to give us a body of *natural philosophy* from the first principles of bodies in general, yet the incomparable Mr. *Newton* has

shewn, how far mathematicks applied to some parts of nature may, upon principles that matter of fact justify, carry us in the knowledge of some, as I may so call them, particular provinces of the incomprehensible universe. And if others could give us so good and clear an account of other parts of *nature,* as he has of this our planetary world, and the most considerable phænomena observable in it, in his admirable book, *Philosophiæ naturalis Principia Mathematica,* we might in time hope to be furnished with more true and certain knowledge in several parts of this stupendous machine, than hitherto we could have expected. And though there are very few that have mathematicks enough to understand his demonstrations, yet the most accurate mathematicians who have examin'd them allowing them to be such, his book will deserve to be read, and give no small light and pleasure to those, who, willing to understand the motions, properties, and operations of the great masses of matter, in this our solar system, will but carefully mind his conclusions, which may be depended on as propositions well proved.

195. This is, in short, what I have thought concerning a young gentleman's studies; wherein it will possibly be wonder'd that I should omit *Greek,* since amongst the *Grecians* is to be found the original as it were, and foundation of all that learning which we have in this part of the world. I grant it so; and will add, that no man can pass for a scholar that is ignorant of the *Greek* tongue. But I am not here considering the education of a profess'd scholar, but of a gentleman, to whom *Latin* and *French,* as the world now goes, is by every one acknowledg'd to be necessary. When he comes to be a man, if he has a mind to carry his studies farther, and look into the *Greek* learning, he will then easily get that tongue himself: and if he has not that inclination, his learning of it under a tutor will be but lost labour, and much of his time and pains spent in that which will be neglected and thrown away as soon as he is at liberty. For how many are there of an hundred, ever amongst scholars themselves, who retain the *Greek* they carried from school; or ever improve it to a familiar reading and perfect understanding of *Greek* authors?

To conclude this part, which concerns a young gentleman's studies, his tutor should remember, that his business is not so much to teach him all that is knowable, as to raise in him a love and esteem of knowledge; and to put him in the right way of knowing and improving himself when he has a mind to it.

The thoughts of a judicious author on the subject of languages, I shall here give the reader, as near as I can, in his own way of expressing them: he says, "One can scarce burden children too much with the knowledge of languages. They are useful to men of all conditions, and they equally open them the entrance, either to the most profound, or the more easy and entertaining parts of learning. If this irksome study be put off to a little more advanced age, young men either have not resolution enough to apply it out of choice or steadiness to carry it on.

And if any one has the gift of perseverance, it is not without the inconvenience of spending that time upon languages, which is destined to other uses: and he confines to the study of words that age of his life that is above it, and requires things; at least it is the losing the best and beautifullest season of one's life. This large foundation of languages cannot be well laid but when every thing makes an easy and deep impression on the mind; when the memory is fresh, ready, and tenacious; when the head and heart are as yet free from cares, passions, and designs; and those on whom the child depends have authority enough to keep him close to a long continued application. I am persuaded that the small number of truly learned, and the multitude of superficial pretenders, is owing to the neglect of this."

I think every body will agree with this observing gentleman, that languages are the proper study of our first years. But 'tis to be consider'd by the parents and tutors, what tongues 'tis fit the child should learn. For it must be confessed, that it is fruitless pains and loss of time, to learn a language which in the course of life that he is designed to, he is never like to make use of, or which one may guess by his temper he will wholly neglect and lose again, as soon as an approach to manhood, setting him free from a governor, shall put him into the hands of his own inclination, which is not likely to allot any of his time to the cultivating the learned tongues, or dispose him to mind any other language but what daily use or some particular necessity shall force upon him.

But yet for the sake of those who are designed to be scholars, I will add what the same author subjoins to make good his foregoing remark. It will deserve to be considered by all who desire to be truly learned, and therefore may be a fit rule for tutors to inculcate and leave with their pupils to guide their future studies.

"The study, *says he,* of the original text can never be sufficiently recommended. 'Tis the shortest, surest, and most agreeable way to all sorts of learning. Draw from the spring-head, and take not things at second hand. Let the writings of the great masters be never laid aside, dwell upon them, settle them in your mind, and cite them upon occasion; make it your business throughly to understand them in their full extent and all their circumstances: acquaint yourself fully with the principles of original authors; bring them to a consistency, and then do you yourself make your deductions. In this state were the first commentators, and do not you rest till you bring yourself to the same. Content not yourself with those borrowed lights, nor guide yourself by their views but where your own fails you and leaves you in the dark. Their explications are not yours, and will give you the slip. On the contrary, your own observations are the product of your own mind, where they will abide and be ready at hand upon all occasions in converse, consultation, and dispute. Lose not the pleasure it is to see that you are not stopp'd in your reading but by difficulties that are invincible; where the commentators and scholiasts themselves are at a stand and have nothing to say. Those copious expositors of other places, who with a vain and pompous overflow of learning poured out on passages plain and easy in themselves, are very free of their words and pains, where there is no need. Convince yourself full by this ordering your studies, that 'tis nothing but men's laziness which hath encouraged pedantry to cram rather than enrich libraries, and to bury good authors under heaps of notes and commentaries, and you will perceive that sloth herein hath acted against itself and its own interest by multiplying reading and enquiries, and encreasing the pains it endeavoured to avoid."

This, tho' it may seem to concern none but direct scholars, is of so great moment for the right ordering of their education and studies, that I hope I shall not be blamed for inserting of it here; especially if it be considered, that it may be of use to gentlemen too, when at any time they have a mind to go deeper than the surface, and get to themselves a solid, satisfactory, and masterly insight in any part of learning.

Order and constancy are said to make the great difference between one man and another: this I am sure, nothing so much clears a learner's way, helps him so much on in it, and makes him go so easy and so far in any enquiry, as a good *method*. His governor should take pains to make him sensible of this, accustom him to order, and teach him *method* in all the applications of his thoughts; shew him wherein it lies, and the advantages of it; acquaint him with the several sorts of it, either from general to particulars, or from particulars to what is more general; exercise him in both of them, and make him see in what cases each different *method* is most proper, and to what ends it best serves.

In history the order of time should govern, in philosophical enquiries that of nature, which in all progression is to go from the place one is then in, to that which joins and lies next to it; and so it is in the mind, from the knowledge it stands possessed of already, to that which lies next, and is coherent to it, and so on to what it aims at, by the simplest and most uncompounded parts it can divide the matter into. To this purpose, it will be of great use to his pupil to accustom him to distinguish well, that is, to have distinct notions, whereever the mind can find any real difference; but as carefully to avoid distinctions in terms, where he has not distinct and different clear ideas.

196. Besides what is to be had from study and books, there are other *accomplishments* necessary for a gentleman, to be got by exercise, and to which time is to be allowed, and for which masters must be had.

Dancing being that which gives *graceful motions* all the life, and above all things manliness, and a becoming confidence to young children, I think it cannot be learned too early, after they are once of an age and strength capable of it. But you must be sure to have a good master, that knows, and can teach, what is graceful and becoming, and what gives a freedom and easiness to all the motions of the body. One that

157

teaches not this, is worse than none at all: natural unfashionableness being much better than apish affected postures; and I think it much more passable, to put off the hat and make a leg like an honest country gentleman than like an ill-fashioned dancing-master. For as for the jigging part, and the figures of dances, I count that little or nothing, farther than as it tends to perfect *graceful carriage.*

197. *Musick* is thought to have some affinity with dancing, and a good hand upon some instruments is by many people mightily valued. But it wastes so much of a young man's time to gain but a moderate skill in it; and engages often in such odd company, that many think it much better spared: and I have amongst men of parts and business so seldom heard any one commended or esteemed for having an excellency in *musick,* that amongst all those things that ever came into the list of accomplishments, I think I may give it the last place. Our short lives will not serve us for the attainment of all things; nor can our minds be always intent on something to be learned. The weakness of our constitutions both of mind and body, requires that we should be often unbent: and he that will make a good use of any part of his life, must allow a large portion of it to *recreation.* At least, this must not be denied to young people; unless whilst you with too much haste make them old, you have the displeasure to set them in their graves or a second childhood sooner than you could wish. And therefore, I think, that the time and pains allotted to serious improvements, should be employed about things of most use and consequence, and that too in the methods the most easy and short that could be at any rate obtained: and perhaps, as I have above said, it would be none of the least secrets of education, to make the exercises of the body and the mind the recreation one to another. I doubt not but that something might be done in it, by a prudent man, that would well consider the temper and inclination of his pupil. For he that is wearied either with study or dancing does not desire presently to go to sleep, but to do something else which may divert and delight him. But this must be always remembered, that nothing can come into the account of *recreation,* that is not done with delight.

198. *Fencing* and *riding the great horse,* are looked upon so necessary parts of breeding, that it would be thought a great *omission* to neglect them; the latter of the two being for the most part to be learned only in great towns, is one of the best exercises for health, which is to be had in those places of ease and luxury: and upon that account makes a fit part of a young gentleman's employment during his abode there. And as far as it conduces to give a man a firm and graceful seat on horseback, and to make him able to teach his horse to stop and turn quick, and to rest on his hanches, is of use to a gentleman both in peace and war. But whether it be of moment enough to be made a business of, and deserve to take up more of his time than should barely for his health be employed at due intervals in some such vigorous exercise, I shall leave to the discretion of parents and tutors; who will do well to remember, in all the parts of education, that most time and

application is to be bestowed on that which is like to be of greatest consequence and frequentest use in the ordinary course and occurrences of that life the young man is designed for.

199. As for *fencing,* it seems to me a good exercise for health, but dangerous to the life; the confidence of their skill being apt to engage in quarrels those that think they have learned to use their swords. This presumption makes them often more touchy than needs on point of honour and slight or no provocations. Young men, in their warm blood, are forward to think they have in vain learned to fence, if they never shew their skill and courage in a duel; and they seem to have reason. But how many sad tragedies that reason has been the occasion of, the tears of many a mother can witness. A man that cannot *fence,* will be more careful to keep out of bullies' and gamesters' company, and will not be half so apt to stand upon punctilios, nor to give affronts, or fiercely justify them when given, which is that which usually makes the quarrel. And when a man is in the field, a moderate skill in fencing rather exposes him to the sword of his enemy than secures him from it. And certainly a man of courage who cannot fence at all and therefore will put all upon one thrust and not stand parrying, has the odds against a moderate fencer, especially if he has skill in wrestling. And therefore, if any provision be to be made against such accidents, and a man be to prepare his son for duels, I had much rather mine should be a good *wrestler* than an ordinary fencer, which is the most a gentleman can attain to in it, unless he will be constantly in the fencing-school and every day exercising. But since fencing and riding the great horse are so generally looked upon as necessary qualifications in the breeding of a gentleman, it will be hard wholly to deny any one of that rank these marks of distinction. I shall leave it therefore to the father to consider, how far the temper of his son and the station he is like to be in, will allow or encourage him to comply with fashions which, having very little to do with civil life, were yet formerly unknown to the most warlike nations, and seem to have added little of force or courage to those who have received them; unless we will think martial skill or prowess have been improved by duelling, with which fencing came into, and with which I presume it will go out of the world.

200. These are my present thoughts concerning *learning* and *accomplishments.* The great business of all is virtue and *wisdom:*

Nullum numen abest si sit Prudentia. Teach him to get a mastery over his inclinations, and *submit his appetite to reason.* This being obtained, and by constant practice settled into habit, the hardest part of the task is over. To bring a young man to this, I know nothing which so much contributes as the love of praise and commendation, which should therefore be instilled into him by all arts imaginable. Make his mind as sensible of credit and shame as may be; and when you have done that, you have put a principle into him, which will influence his actions when you are not by, to which the fear of a little smart of a rod is not comparable, and which will be the proper stock whereon afterwards to graff the true principles of morality and religion.

Sections 201–210

201. I have one thing more to add, which as soon as I mention I shall run the danger of being suspected to have forgot what I am about, and what I have above written concerning education all tending towards a gentleman's calling, with which a trade seems wholly inconsistent. And yet I cannot forbear to say, I would have him *learn a trade, a manual trade;* nay two or three, but one more particularly.

202. The busy inclination of children being always to be directed to something that may be useful to them, the advantages proposed from what they are set about may be considered of two kinds: 1. Where the skill itself that is got by exercise is worth the having. Thus skill not only in languages and learned sciences, but in painting, turning, gardening, tempering and working in iron, and all other useful arts is worth the having. 2. Where the exercise itself, without any consideration, is necessary or useful for health. Knowledge in some things is so necessary to be got by children whilst they are young, that some part of their time is to be allotted to their improvement in them, though those employments contribute nothing at all to their health. Such are reading and writing and all other sedentary studies for the cultivating of the mind, which unavoidably take up a great part of a gentleman's time, quite from their cradles. *Other manual arts,* which are both got and exercised by labour, do many of them by that exercise not only increase our dexterity and skill, but contribute to our health too, especially such as employ us in the open air. In these, then, health and improvement may be join'd together; and of these should some fit ones be chosen, to be made the recreations of one whose chief business is with books and study. In this choice the age and inclination of the person is to be considered, and constraint always to be avoided in bringing him to it. For command and force may often create, but can never cure, an aversion: and whatever any one is brought to by compulsion, he will leave as soon as he can, and be little profited and less recreated by, whilst he is at it.

203. That which of all others would please me best, would be a *painter,* were there not an argument or two against it not easy to be answered. First, ill painting is one of the worst things in the world; and to attain a tolerable degree of skill in it, requires too much of a man's time. If he has a natural inclination to it, it will endanger the neglect of all other more useful studies to give way to that; and if he have no inclination to it, all the time, pains and money shall be employed in it, will be thrown away to no purpose. Another reason why I am not for

painting in a gentleman, is, because it is a sedentary recreation, which more employs the mind than the body. A gentleman's more serious employment I look on to be study; and when that demands relaxation and refreshment, it should be in some exercise of the body, which unbends the thought, and confirms the health and strength. For these two reasons I am not for *painting*.

204. In the next place, for a country gentleman I should propose one, or rather both these, *viz. Gardening* or *husbandry* in general, and working in wood, as a *carpenter, joiner,* or *turner,* these being fit and healthy recreations for a man of study or business. For since the mind endures not to be constantly employed in the same thing or way, and sedentary or studious men should have some exercise, that at the same time might divert their minds and employ their bodies, I know none that could do it better for a country gentleman than these two; the one of them affording him exercise when the weather or season keeps him from the other. Besides that, by being skill'd in the one of them, he will be able to govern and teach his gardener; by the other, contrive and make a great many things both of delight and use: though these I propose not as the chief end of his labour, but as temptations to it; diversion from his other more serious thoughts and employments by useful and healthy manual exercise being what I chiefly aim at in it.

205. The great men among the antients understood very well how to reconcile manual labour with affairs of state, and thought it no lessening to their dignity to make the one the recreation to the other. That indeed which seems most generally to have employed and diverted their spare hours, was agriculture. *Gideon* among the *Jews* was taken from threshing, as well as *Cincinnatus* amongst the *Romans* from the plough, to command the armies of their countries against their enemies; and 'tis plain their dexterous handling of the flayl or the plough, and being good workmen with these tools, did not hinder their skill in arms, nor make them less able in the arts of war or government. They were great captains and statesmen as well as husbandmen. *Cato Major,* who had with great reputation born all the great offices of the commonwealth, has left us an evidence under his own hand, how much he was versed in country affairs; and, as I remember, *Cyrus* thought *gardening* so little beneath the dignity and grandeur of a throne, that he shew'd *Xenophon* a large field of fruit-trees all of his own planting. The records of antiquity, both among *Jews* and *Gentiles,* are full of instances of this kind, if it were necessary to recommend useful recreations by examples.

206. Nor let it be thought that I mistake, when I call these or the like exercises of manual arts, *diversions* or *recreations:* for *recreation* is not being idle (as every one may observe) but easing the wearied part by change of business: and he that thinks *diversion* may not lie in hard and painful labour, forgets the early rising, hard riding, heat, cold and hunger of huntsmen, which is yet known to be the constant recreation of men of the greatest condition. *Delving, planting, inoculating,* or any the like profitable employments, would be no less a *diversion* than any

of the idle sports in fashion, if men could but be brought to delight in them, which custom and skill in a trade will quickly bring any one to do. And I doubt not but there are to be found those, who being frequently called to cards or any other play by those they could not refuse, have been more tired with these *recreations* than with any the most serious employment of life, though the play has been such as they have naturally had no aversion to, and with which they could willingly sometimes divert themselves.

207. Play, wherein persons of condition, especially ladies, waste so much of their time, is a plain instance to me that men cannot be perfectly idle; they must be doing something; for how else could they sit so many hours toiling at that which generally gives more vexation than delight to people whilst they are actually engag'd in it? 'Tis certain, gaming leaves no satisfaction behind it to those who reflect when it is over, and it no way profits either body or mind: as to their estates, if it strike so deep as to concern them, it is a *trade* then, and not a *recreation*, wherein few that have any thing else to live on thrive: and at best, a thriving gamester has but a poor trade on't, who fills his pockets at the price of his reputation.

Recreation belongs not to people who are strangers to business, and are not wasted and wearied with the employment of their calling. The skill should be, so to order their time of recreation, that it may relax and refresh the part that has been exercised and is tired, and yet do something which besides the present delight and ease, may produce what will afterwards be profitable. It has been nothing but the vanity and pride of greatness and riches, that has brought unprofitable and dangerous *pastimes* (as they are called) into fashion, and persuaded people into a belief, that the learning or putting their hands to any thing that was useful, could not be a *diversion* fit for a gentleman. This has been that which has given *cards, dice* and *drinking* so much credit in the world: and a great many throw away their spare hours in them, through the prevalency of custom, and want of some better employment to fill up the vacancy of leisure, more than from any real delight is to be found in them. They cannot bear the dead weight of unemployed time lying upon their hands, nor the uneasiness it is to do nothing at all: and having never learned any laudable manual art wherewith to divert themselves, they have recourse to those foolish or ill ways in use, to help off their time, which a rational man, till corrupted by custom, could find very little pleasure in.

208. I say not this, that I would never have a young gentleman accommodate himself to the innocent *diversions* in fashion amongst those of his age and condition. I am so far from having him austere and morose to that degree, that I would persuade him to more than ordinary complaisance for all the gaieties and *diversions* of those he converses with, and be averse or testy in nothing they should desire of him, that might become a gentleman and an honest man. Though as to *cards* and *dice*, I think the safest and best way is never to learn any play upon

them, and so to be incapacitated for those dangerous temptations and incroaching wasters of useful time. But allowance being made for *idle and jovial conversation* and all fashionable becoming recreations; I say, a young man will have time enough from his serious and main business, to learn almost any *trade*. 'Tis want of application, and not of leisure, that men are not skilful in more arts than one; and an hour in a day, constantly employed in such a way of *diversion*, will carry a man in a short time a great deal farther than he can imagine: which, if it were of no other use but to drive the common, vicious, useless, and dangerous pastimes out of fashion, and to shew there was no need of them, would deserve to be encouraged. If men from their youth were weaned from that sauntring humour wherein some out of custom let a good part of their lives run uselessly away, without either business or recreation, they would find time enough to acquire *dexterity and skill in hundreds of things*, which, though remote from their proper callings, would not at all interfere with them. And therefore, I think, for this, as well as other reasons before-mentioned, a lazy, listless humour that idly dreams away the days, is of all others the least to be indulged or permitted in young people. It is the proper state of one sick and out of order in his health, and is tolerable in nobody else of what age or condition soever.

209. To the arts above-mentioned may be added *perfuming, varnishing, graving,* and several sorts of working in *iron, brass,* and *silver;* and if, as it happens to most young gentlemen, that a considerable part of his time be spent in a great town, he may learn to cut, polish, and set *precious stones,* or employ himself in grinding and polishing *optical glasses.* Amongst the great variety there is of ingenious *manual arts,* 'twill be impossible that no one should be found to please and delight him, unless he be either idle or debauched, which is not to be supposed in a right way of education. And since he cannot be always employ'd in study, reading, and conversation, there will be many an hour, besides what his exercises will take up, which, if not spent this way, will be spent worse. For I conclude, a young man will seldom desire to sit perfectly still and idle; or, if he does, 'tis a fault that ought to be mended.

210. But if his mistaken parents, frighted with the disgraceful names of *mechanick* and *trade,* shall have an aversion to any thing of this kind in their children; yet there is one thing relating to trade, which, when they consider, they will think absolutely necessary for their sons to learn.

Merchants' accompts, tho' a science not likely to help a gentleman to get an estate, yet possibly there is not any thing of more use and efficacy, to make him preserve the estate he has. 'Tis seldom observed, that he keeps an accompt of his income and expenses, and thereby has constantly under view the course of his domestick affairs, lets them run to ruin: and I doubt not but many a man gets behind-hand before he is aware, or runs farther on when he is once in, for want of this care, or the skill to do it. I would therefore advise all gentlemen to learn perfectly *merchants' accompts,* and not to think it is a skill that belongs not to them, because it has received its name from, and has been chiefly practised by men of traffick.

Sections 211-217

211. When my young master has once got the skill of *keeping accounts* (which is a business of reason more than arithmetick) perhaps it will not be amiss that his father from thenceforth require him to do it in all his concernments. Not that I would have him set down every pint of wine or play that costs him money; the general name of expenses will serve for such things well enough: nor would I have his father look so narrowly into these accompts, as to take occasion from thence to criticise on his expences; he must remember that he himself was once a young man, and not forget the thoughts he had then, nor the right his son has to have the same, and to have allowance made for them. If therefore I would have the young gentleman oblig'd to keep an account, it is not at all to have that way a check upon his expenses (for what the father allows him, he ought to let him be fully master of) but only, that he might be brought early into the custom of doing it, and that it might be made familiar and habitual to him betimes, which will be so useful and necessary to be constantly practised the whole course of his life. A noble *Venetian,* whose son wallowed in the plenty of his father's riches, finding his son's expenses grow very high and extravagant, ordered his cashier to let him have for the future no more money than what he should count when he received it. This one would think no great restraint to a young gentleman's expenses; who could freely have as much money as he would tell. But yet this, to one that was used to nothing but the pursuit of his pleasures, prov'd a very great trouble, which at last ended in this sober and advantageous reflection: if it be so much pains to me barely to count the money I would spend, what labour and pains did it cost my ancestors, not only to count, but get it? This rational thought, suggested by this little pains impos'd upon him, wrought so effectually upon his mind, that it made him take up, and from that time forwards prove a good husband. This, at least, every body must allow, that nothing is likelier to keep a man within compass than the having constantly before his eyes the state of his affairs in a regular course of *accompt.*

212. The last part usually in education is *travel,* which is commonly thought to finish the work, and complete the gentleman. I confess *travel* into foreign countries has great advantages, but the time usually chosen to send young men abroad, is, I think, of all other, that which renders their least capable of reaping those *advantages.* Those which are propos'd, as to the main of them, may be reduced to these two: first, language, secondly, an improvement in wisdom and prudence, by seeing men, and conversing with people of tempers, customs and ways

of living, different from one another, and especially from those of his parish and neighbourhood. But from sixteen to one and twenty, which is the ordinary *time of travel,* men are, of all their lives, the least suited to these improvements. The first season to get foreign languages, and form the tongue to their true accents, I should think, should be from seven to fourteen or sixteen, and then too a tutor with them is useful and necessary, who may with those languages teach them other things. But to put them out of their parents' view at a great distance under a governor, when they think themselves to be too much men to be governed by others, and yet have not prudence and experience enough to govern themselves, what is it, but to expose them to all the greatest dangers of their whole life, when they have the least fence and guard against them? 'Till that boiling boisterous part of life comes in, it may be hoped the tutor may have some authority: neither the stubbornness of age, nor the temptation or examples of others, can take him from his tutor's conduct till fifteen or sixteen; but then, when he begins to comfort himself with men, and thinks himself one; when he comes to relish and pride himself in manly vices, and thinks it a shame to be any longer under the controul and conduct of another, what can be hoped from even the most careful and discreet governor, when neither he has power to compel, nor his pupil a disposition to be persuaded; but on the contrary, has the advice of warm blood and prevailing fashion, to hearken to the temptations of his companions, just as wise as himself, rather than to the persuasions of his tutor, who is now looked on as an enemy to his freedom? And when is a man so like to miscarry, as when at the same time he is both raw and unruly? This is the season of all his life that most requires the eye and authority of his parents and friends to govern it. The flexibleness of the former part of a man's age, not yet grown up to be headstrong, makes it more governable and safe; and in the afterpart, reason and foresight begin a little to take place, and mind a man of his safety and improvement. The time therefore I should think the fittest for a young gentleman to be *sent abroad,* would be, either when he is younger, under a tutor, whom he might be the better for; or when he is some years older, without a governor; when he is of age to govern himself, and make observations of what he finds in other countries worthy his notice, and that might be of use to him after his return; and when too, being throughly acquainted with the laws and fashions, the natural and moral advantages and defects of his own country, he has something to exchange with those abroad, from whose conversation he hoped to reap any knowledge.

213. [Wanting].

214. The ordering of travel otherwise, is that, I imagine, which makes so many young gentlemen come back so little improved by it. And if they do bring home with them any knowledge of the places and people they have seen, it is often an admiration of the worst and vainest practices they met with abroad; retaining a relish and memory of those things wherein their liberty took its first swing, rather than of what should make them better and wiser after their return. And indeed how

can it be otherwise, going abroad at the age they do under the care of another, who is to provide their necessaries, and make their observations for them? Thus under the shelter and pretence of a governor, thinking themselves excused from standing upon their own legs or being accountable for their own conduct, they very seldom trouble themselves with enquiries or making useful observations of their own. Their thoughts run after play and pleasure, wherein they take it as a lessening to be controll'd; but seldom trouble themselves to examine the designs, observe the address, and consider the arts, tempers, and inclinations of men they meet with; that so they may know how to comport themselves towards them. Here he that travels with them is to screen them; get them out when they have run themselves into the briars; and in all their miscarriages be answerable for them.

215. I confess, the knowledge of men is so great a skill, that it is not to be expected a young man should presently be perfect in it. But yet his *going abroad* is to little purpose, if *travel* does not sometimes open his eyes, make him cautious and wary, and accustom him to look beyond the outside, and, under the inoffensive guard of a civil and obliging carriage, keep himself free and safe in his conversation with strangers and all sorts of people without forfeiting their good opinion. He that is sent out to *travel* at the age, and with the thoughts of a man designing to improve himself, may get into the conversation and acquaintance of persons of condition where he comes; which, tho' a thing of most advantage to a gentleman that travels, yet I ask, amongst our young men that go abroad under tutors, what one is there of an hundred, that ever visits any person of quality? Much less makes an acquaintance with such, from whose conversation he may learn what is good breeding in that country, and what is worth observation in it; tho' from such persons it is, one may learn more in one day, than in a year's rambling from one inn to another. Nor indeed, is it to be wondered; for men of worth and parts will not easily admit the familiarity of boys who yet need the care of a tutor; tho' a young gentleman and stranger, appearing like a man, and shewing a desire to inform himself in the customs, manners, laws, and government of the country he is in, will find welcome assistance and entertainment amongst the best and most knowing persons every where, who will be ready to receive, encourage and countenance, an ingenuous and inquisitive foreigner.

216. This, how true soever it be, will not I fear alter the custom, which has cast the time of travel upon the worst part of a man's life; but for reasons not taken from their improvement. The young lad must not be ventured abroad at eight or ten, for fear of what may happen to the tender child, tho' he then runs ten times less risque than at sixteen or eighteen. Nor must he stay at home till that dangerous, heady age be over, because he must be back again by one and twenty, to marry and propagate. The father cannot stay any longer for the portion, nor the mother for a new set of babies to play with; and so my young master, whatever comes on it, must have a wife look'd out for him by that time he is of age; tho' it would be no prejudice to his strength, his parts, or

his issue, if it were respited for some time, and he had leave to get, in years and knowledge, the start a little of his children, who are often found to tread too near upon the heels of their fathers, to the no great satisfaction either of son or father. But the young gentleman being got within view of matrimony, 'tis time to leave him to his mistress.

217. Tho' I am now come to a conclusion of what obvious remarks have suggested to me concerning education, I would not have it thought that I look on it as a just treatise on this subject. There are a thousand other things that may need consideration; especially if one should take in the various tempers, different inclinations, and particular defaults, that are to be found in children, and prescribe proper remedies. The variety is so great that it would require a volume; nor would that reach it. Each man's mind has some peculiarity, as well as his face, that distinguishes him from all others; and there are possibly scarce two children who can be conducted by exactly the same method. Besides that, I think a prince, a nobleman, and an ordinary gentleman's son, should have different ways of breeding. But having had here only some general views in reference to the main end and aims in education, and those designed for a gentleman's son, whom, being then very little, I considered only as white paper, or wax, to be moulded and fashioned as one pleases; I have touched little more than those heads which I judged necessary for the breeding of a young gentleman of his condition in general; and have now published these my occasional thoughts with this hope, that tho' this be far from being a complete treatise on this subject, or such as that every one may find what will just fit his child in it, yet it may give some small light to those, whose concern for their dear little ones makes them so irregularly bold, that they dare venture to consult their own reason in the education of their children, rather than wholly to rely upon old custom.